# THE
# HEALING
# ALPHABET

## *26* Empowering
## Ways to Enrich Your Life

Printed in the United States of America

# The Healing Alphabet

## 26 *Empowering*
## *Ways to Enrich Your Life*

Rossana Snee, MFT

Los Angeles, California

*Dedicated to my mother, Sylvia Perez, who never lost faith that this book would one day step out into the world and make a difference.*

# Acknowledgments

A very special thanks to Erin Littlewood, without whose help this book would probably not be published. She always believed in its magic and was instrumental in the editing process.

A heartfelt thank you to my husband, Joe Snee, who tirelessly read my manuscript until the last typo was caught and deleted.

A huge thank you to John Lynch, my first born, for helping me with everything—from getting my manuscript ready for publishing to being available for brainstorming ideas and believing in my book's eventual success.

A special thank you to Christopher J. Lynch, who was always willing and happy to answer all my questions when I didn't know what the heck I was doing in readying my book for publication.

And to the rest of my amazing family ... my father, Rolando Perez, whose love and positivity feeds my soul; my son Joshua Snee, who volunteered his time to run errands for me just so that I could keep on working; and to all my friends who've been an unending source of support.

A great big THANK YOU to you all!

❖ To the right choices that lie within us ❖

# CONTENTS

# Introduction

You have the power to **CHOOSE** a good life. Do you know how? Allow me to show you the way. A good life lies open before you if you are willing to look, learn, and do. Available to you, then, are numerous choices that can enrich your life and the lives of others. Look around you. Your past choices got you where you are today. Are you happy where you are? Would you like to be happier and more satisfied with your life?

Some of you believe that you don't have a choice in whatever situation you find yourself—that under your "special" circumstances, it is impossible to do anything different. However, you **ALWAYS** have a choice, no matter what the circumstances or the situation. Do not let appearances deceive you. Within every challenging situation, the opportunity to choose becomes even more significant and meaningful—the springboard to growth and enlightenment. Paths previously unexplored can become the gateway to a new and better life. Therefore, the option to choose is always there for you. In **The Healing Alphabet: 26 Empowering Ways to Enrich Your Life**, I present alternative choices that, if made, can help you become the best you can be.

Allow this book to guide you on your way. **CHOOSE** to make your life better, to exercise your freedom, to fulfill your potential, and to reach your goals. When you realize you have choices, you empower yourself. When you empower yourself, you take responsibility for your life; you become the driver, not the passenger. Even though some choices are difficult, they are the key to changing your life. Life offers endless possibilities to flourish. I hope you find the joy and happiness due to you all.

—Rossana Snee, MFT

# Accept

*Life without acceptance is a life with limitations.*

Acceptance is freedom, as long as you remember that people come in different models. Some people do hurtful things. Some people act or look differently.

The people who do hurtful things require acceptance but do not need to be accepted into your life. Perhaps it is your hope to change someone into being a kinder, more loving and honest person. It's difficult enough to change yourself, let alone someone else. Can you imagine someone saying, "Well, if John Doe were alive, he'd be perfect!" Most people can change others about as easily as they can change John Doe's state of repose. It is impossible. In dealing with hurtful people, accept that you can't change them, but don't allow yourself to be victimized by them. Love yourself enough to accept that the person cannot be changed and move on. You *never* have to accept any type of abuse.

With people who look or act differently than you do, realize that DIFFERENT doesn't equal BAD; it just equals DIFFERENT. You may be unwilling to accept others because of their:

1) Appearance

2) Background

3) Ethnicity

4) Age

5) Economic Status

6) Weight

STOP! Learn to accept those differences and to value people's uniqueness. No one really knows anyone else's life path and challenges. In choosing to accept people's differences, you open up your world. You stop being judge and jury. Remember also to accept your own differences.

I used to work with a client who had lost his thumb in a job-related accident. He couldn't accept the fact that he was no longer "normal." This caused him a great deal of anguish. Not wanting to be rejected by his peers, he worked hard at covering up his hand, pretending that his thumb was still there whenever he went out in public. Peace for him would only be possible if he learned to accept his situation.

*Accept that life isn't perfect,*
*but the best you can make it.*

If it's not others or yourself that you have a difficult time accepting, how about:

* A **COMPLIMENT**

Maybe you have difficulty accepting an admiring remark. Someone says, "Hey, that's a great outfit on you." Your response, "This old thing?" Or let's say you've just painted a portrait and a friend says,

"That's amazing! You're really good!" You might say, "Oh, it's not that good. Notice the eyes aren't even. I'm just a beginner!" Next time someone pays you a compliment, try saying, "Thank you for noticing." Pay attention to how that makes you feel. The inability to accept a compliment may very well be related to feeling unworthy, or unlovable; maybe you were fed false messages growing up. If that's the case, someone paying you a compliment won't feel like a truth when you hear it, even though it may very well be.

## * An **APOLOGY**

What do you do when someone does or says something that hurts you? If they apologize, accept the apology gracefully. Forgive them. LET THE HURT GO. Holding on will only hurt YOU. Don't make them beg for mercy, or keep rubbing it in their face. If Johnny says he's truly sorry for being late and missing the movie, accept it. Don't start with, "I can't believe you were late again; you're unbelievable. How do you even make it to work on a daily basis? Geez!" Just let go! It's not the end of the world. Everyone makes blunders now and then.

## * **MONEY**

Do you allow yourself to accept financial help? You may feel you can't or that it shows weakness. My dad is one of those people. He's quick to help everyone else, but he has a difficult time accepting it when it comes to himself. My husband and I recently bought two recliners, one for him and one for my mom. His was so old, it actually had tape on one of the armrests to hold it together. When I told him the great news, his response was, "Oh no! You shouldn't have spent the money! You should have saved it for yourself." I smiled and walked away. You can't give without receiving and vice versa. It goes both ways. Realize that everyone needs help from time to time. Don't let pride stand in the way. Accept the help. Then help someone else.

\* Well-meaning **ADVICE**

How do you respond when someone gives you advice? Do you resist? Immediately shut down? It's a good idea to stay open. You might just learn something new. Not all advice is an attack on your person. If you take it that way, you might actually be dealing with leftover pain—harsh criticism from your past. You don't have to agree with everything you hear. Accept what feels right. Discard the rest. It really is good to hear someone else's perspective. They may have a different take—one to which you are oblivious—that could really open your eyes to something spectacular.

\* **YOU**

Learn to accept who you are. Accept the things that can't be changed. Change the things you can. Choose to do so. You are **BEAUTIFUL**. You are **UNIQUE**. You are **MAGNIFICENT**. There is no one else like you!

"Happiness can exist only in acceptance."

~George Orwell

Free yourself! **CHOOSE** to *ACCEPT*.

*** 

### *EXERCISE*

This week, accept something you've had trouble accepting before.

Some examples:

1) An unexpected gift. Express your gratitude.

2) A difference in someone else. View people like flowers. Differences don't make a flower any less valuable; they're valuable because of their differences.

3) Yourself (without criticism). Change the tape in your head that continuously puts you down. Before you say there's no tape in your head, listen throughout the day at the things you tell yourself. You might be surprised.

4) The flaws in others. Who's perfect? No one.

5) _____

(Can you think of something else to accept?)

# Behave

*It is the way you behave that is always on display, not your intentions.*

READY ON THE SET ... TAKE ONE—ACTION! Or you can just as easily say, READY ON THE SET ... TAKE ONE—BEHAVE! Behavior is:

- ACTION taken

- Something VISIBLE

When you look around, what are some of the behaviors you notice? How do *you* behave? At home? At work? In public? In private? The way you behave tells the true story about who you are. What kind of story do you want to tell? Only you can choose.

Behave so that your character is ruled by goodness and integrity. Any ACTION TAKEN by you, big or small, is what defines your character. Your intentions do not. You could have the best of intentions, but if you don't follow through, nothing comes of it.

Here's an example: Your sister lets you know that although Aunt Rose is home from the hospital, she is still feeling weak. You sympathize and think, *I'm going to buy Aunt Rose some flowers and pay her a visit*. Those are very caring intentions. On the way out, you realize it's three o'clock and your favorite talk show is about to start. Just then your best friend calls and invites you to the movies. You record your show and accept your friend's invite. After all, how can you pass up Jake Gyllenhaal? After the movie, you go out for coffee. You have a blast catching up. Remember Aunt Rose? Your intentions, though kind, weren't followed up with action.

Now imagine this *action-oriented* scenario: Your sister calls and lets you know Aunt Rose is home from the hospital. You immediately dress, record your show, and take a rain check from your friend. On the way to Aunt Rose's, you stop by the flower shop and buy her a beautiful bouquet. When you arrive at Aunt Rose's, you feel great to see her face light up at your unexpected visit. In this case, you followed through with your intentions. You gave them life. *It is movement that creates energy. Words alone cannot. Thoughts alone cannot. Only movement can.*

*It is the act by which you are judged, not the thought.*

Behavior is SOMETHING VISIBLE, on display for all to see. Are you proud of your behavior? Would you like to behave differently? If you were being recorded right now, would you change your behavior in any way, or would you keep it the same? If you said you'd change it, why? The fact that you *can* change your behavior is truly empowering. It lets you know that you have control over what you do. Isn't that great to know?

British philosopher and social scientist Jeremy Bentham designed the "Panopticon"—a type of prison, circularly shaped, that allowed its whole prison population to be visually isolated from each other, yet continuously watched by a small group of guards. The Panopticon was used as a means to punitively control the prisoners. Bentham believed that if someone were being watched all the time, or if you got them to believe they were, their behavior (i.e., personality) could be altered for the better. This is because most of us behave differently when we think we're being watched— proof that behavior can be chosen.

Most of you tend to be on your best behavior if you believe you're being observed; but if you think you're not, that's another story.

On a walk once, I saw someone in a nearby car dump all of his fast food remains onto the street. I was appalled. I had seen him, but he hadn't realized he'd had a witness to his unconscionable behavior. I'm sure if he'd known I was only a few feet away, he may not have gone through with his trash dumping. Just like the prisoners exposed to the Panopticon, his behavior would more than likely have been different. Either way, it would have been his choice.

Here's another example: Have you ever been in the middle of an out-of-control yelling match with someone? "YOU PIG! HOW COULD YOU HAVE DONE THIS TO ME? YOU'LL PAY FOR THIS, YOU LOUSY SCUMBAG." Then the phone rings. You answer (in a calm, pleasant voice), "Hello! Oh, hi, Laura. Nice to hear from you! Things are great.

How about you?" The transformation is remarkable. How does this happen? It's simple: You can choose your behavior at any time. You may not be able to choose how you feel, but you can certainly choose your reaction to it.

A Newcastle University team (RxPG), placed an "honesty box"—a method of payment whereby it is left up to the customer to pay a specified price for services rendered—under a poster with eyes on it. The results? Three times the regular amount was put in the box, as opposed to when the box was under a poster with flowers. People generally want to be thought of as honest and good by others (hence why the eyes made a difference). They associated that poster with being watched. But it all goes back to choice. If you can put more money with the eyes staring at you, you can still do the same with the flowers. It's your choice!

The way you behave is important. What do you want others to see? How do you define yourself? Do you behave kindly, honestly, and with integrity? CHOOSE wisely. Someone is almost always WATCHING!

> "Whenever you do a thing,
> act as if the world were watching."
> ~Thomas Jefferson

# CHOOSE to B*EHAVE* admirably.

## *EXERCISE*

Examine the way you behave for a day. Pretend your life is being recorded. Remember that 1998 film *The Truman Show*, starring Jim Carrey? His whole life was being recorded with hidden cameras. Imagine that *you* have an audience, that your life is on display. The world is watching. How will you behave? And what if you behaved like that all the time?

# Celebrate

*Celebrate the little things;*
*they make the big ones count.*

*Kool and the Gang* had it right with their 1980s hit song "Celebration" about celebrating good times. While you don't actually have to get up and dance in order to celebrate good times, it's not a bad idea. Some of you, focused only on the daily drudgeries of life, may think that you have nothing to celebrate. If this sounds familiar, take a minute to answer the following questions:

1) Did you wake up this morning to a brand-new day?

2) Did you interact with a loved one?

3) Were you able to eat or drink something?

4) Do you have a roof over your head?

5) Do you have a job, or the ability to look for one?

6) Are you able to hear and smell the coffee brewing? Feel the sun's warmth on your face?

If you answered "yes" to at least one or more of these questions, you have something to celebrate.

Many of you concentrate all of your energies on the **PROBLEM OF THE DAY**, whichever one it happens to be at the time. And believe me, there's always one lurking, not unlike a stalker hell-bent on watching your every move. Perhaps you carelessly ignore the countless little things that, when added up, make up the content of your life. Life, after all, *is* a series of events—some little, some big—all happening each minute of every day.

Are there some things you take for granted? I certainly know I do. How about a memory that brings a smile to your face, or creates a tingle in your belly? There are people who suffer from Alzheimer's who don't even know who their loved ones are. Celebrate remembering! How about freedom? There are countries like Cuba, where I was born, in which people aren't allowed to express themselves and are punished severely, sometimes killed, if they do. Celebrate your freedom!

It's wonderful to celebrate special events in your lives, such as birthdays, marriages, anniversaries, promotions, etc. Clearly, these big events are cause for celebration. But those events are just the icing on the cake. Before the icing goes on, however, there first has to be a cake.

Let me give you an example: You're about to graduate. Whether it's from a high school, a vocational school, or a university, it doesn't matter; all are cause for celebration. The graduation is the icing. The cake is all the time spent attending classes, reading textbooks, writing essays, taking tests, etc. Are those not an even greater cause for celebration? That's what took all the work. So why not celebrate the fact you're in school? Or that you finished an essay on time? That you finished an essay at all? These may seem like insignificant, little things, but without them, you would not be graduating.

Celebrating life is your answer to what life has to offer. Don't disregard anything as insignificant. Everything counts.

*To celebrate life is to honor it.*

Celebrating life can be fun and simple. All you have to do is notice everything you do all day long—the things you fail to appreciate. It could be something as simple as drinking a glass of water. That, in and of itself, is cause for celebration. You might be thinking, *Celebrate drinking water*? *That's crazy*! If you think that's crazy, try going without water for a few days. My dad is on dialysis three times a week. He can't drink fluids. All he can do is take tiny sips here and there. It's very tough, especially in the summer. He always says, "Rossana, be happy you can drink water; it's so hard not being able to." So next time you take a sip of water and quench your thirst, think twice and CELEBRATE!

*Life is a series of moments*
*linked by every breath you take.*

There are no unimportant moments in life. Each moment is valuable, for it carries you to the next.

There is even a purpose to the moments you consider painful.

When my husband and I were first married, we ended up in family counseling due to adjustment problems with his son/my stepson. Those were very trying and difficult times. Yet the fact that we ended up in therapy motivated me to go back to school and become a Marriage & Family Therapist. Had we not had problems and gone to counseling, I may not have become a therapist, doing something I love—helping people. It was those very challenging moments that caused me to stretch and to move our family to the next level.

The difficult times offer you the opportunity to start anew, to choose a different path. Challenging periods in your life can strengthen you. You can learn to rise above. Step out of the rubble and rebuild. Celebrate the fact you have that opportunity.

"Life should not only be lived, it should be celebrated."

~Osho

# CHOOSE to CELEBRATE in every way!

***

## *EXERCISE*

Today, celebrate something that you might be taking for granted. How about:

1) The ability to get around, whether it is by walking or with the help of a wheelchair or walker.

2) The gift of sight, hearing, or feeling.

3) The ability to open a jar.

4) The luxury of sleep.

5) The freedom to communicate.

6) Friends and family.

You get the picture. Choose to celebrate anything, BIG or small. Start today.

# **D**are

*Dare to be yourself! Accept no imitations!*

YOU. I dare you to be **YOU**! Would that be an easy or difficult task? Who are you, really? There is the YOU people see, the YOU you pretend to be, the YOU you'd like to be, and the true YOU buried somewhere in the throes of it all. Why so many YOUs?

From the moment you're born, you learn about limitations, dos and don'ts, what *not* to do, and whom *not* to be. The negative messages pour in on a daily basis, fill you up, and eventually spill out, spreading to all aspects of your life. See if any of these messages sound familiar:

"That's not good enough; try again."

"You have way too much energy. Settle down."

"Don't just sit there—do something!"

"Stay inside the lines."

"You are so clumsy!"

"Don't touch that; you'll break it!"

While sitting next to a woman whose son was taking ice-skating lessons, this is what I heard: "Is that as fast as you can go? Go faster. Can't you do any better? Your leg is not high enough. Watch out! Go away! Don't come back until you do it right. Leave me alone. Wiggle more. Spin faster." It was a verbal beating unlike any I'd heard in a long time. The poor boy could do no right. In his mind, he was already a loser. What messages did you hear growing up? Do you still hear them in your mind like a worn-out recording? Was it okay for you to be you? Or did you have to hide a part of yourself to feel loved and accepted? If it wasn't okay to be you, it's not too late. Dare to express yourself in the way your heart desires—without, of course, expressing yourself in a way that would be hurtful to others. (I know you know that, but I thought I'd throw that in for good measure.)

Perhaps you take on roles in order to fit in. You might be afraid that if you don't, no one will like you. The problem with role-playing is that you'll attract only those who know and accept your false self. Take the following **IS IT REALLY YOU?** test:

1) Do you say things because it's what you think others want to hear?

2) Are you afraid to wear something because of what someone else might say?

3) Do you keep from doing something you love because someone might not like it?

4) Do you act a certain way because that's what everyone expects?

5) Do you say "yes" when you really want to say "no"?

How did you do? Did you answer "yes" to any of those questions? If so, you might be compromising

YOU. And what a great gift YOU are! Imagine not having to pretend and not having to remember who you're not.

When you dare to be yourself, you're admitting that you are **WISE**—**W**onderful. **I**rreplaceable. **S**pecial. **E**xciting. Dare to accept this truth. Disregard the lies you may have heard repeatedly since birth. Disregard the lies you've repeatedly told yourself. You were created in the likeness of perfection, no matter what anybody else tells you.

*Dare to be yourself without pretenses.*

Why is it that so many people suffer from low self-esteem? Were they born that way? I don't think so. Imagine a doctor delivering a baby and saying, "We've got a problem! Nurse, call in the psychologist STAT; this baby's got low self-esteem." Low self-esteem is not something with which you're born. Like a seed, it's planted. As you grow, the seed sprouts, creating havoc and causing insecurity and unhappiness. Daring to be yourself is affirming, "I like who I am, and like it or not, that's who I'm going to be."

What steps can you take to be YOU?

1) Dare to **DISCOVER** who you are. Explore your likes, dislikes, and feelings.

2) Dare to **BE** who you really are. Stop pretending. Take off your mask.

3) Dare to **LOVE** who you are, unconditionally. You're worth loving.

In the beginning, you might feel insecure and at odds with yourself. Be patient. Anything new requires practice. It's scary being real, especially if you have deep fears about being rejected. That's natural. Baby steps are the way to go.

Your true self is in there. Bring *IT* out of hiding. Set the fear aside. If necessary, get some help— someone who can guide you along, walk with you as you grow into who you're supposed to be. Stop pretending to be someone you're not simply to gain acceptance. The true you sometimes leaks out when you least expect it. Become aware of those moments. How? You'll feel as though everything is right with the world. Instead of fear, you'll feel peace. In that instant, what you feel = who you are; no pretenses are in place. Embrace those moments. Aim for more like that. Make it a habit to be YOU! It's one you won't want to break.

"Valor grows by daring, fear by holding back."

~Publilius Syrus

I double-dog **D**ARE you! **CHOOSE** to be you!

***

## *EXERCISE*

DARE to:

1) Be yourself at the risk of looking foolish. For example, get up and dance and don't worry about who's watching.

2) Have a different opinion. And voice it. Don't let timidity stop you. Whether you believe it or not, your voice IS important.

3) Step out of your comfort zone. How will you know you've stepped out? You'll feel a trickle of fear/excitement, a seed of doubt, and a voice telling you, "GET BACK IN THE ZONE!"

4) Say "no" without feeling guilty. If there's something you don't want to do, don't. Just because someone asks you, it doesn't mean you have to. Here's an example: All your friends are going to see *Deadpool*. As much as you love Ryan Reynolds, you don't enjoy graphic nudity in movies. Your friends push you to say "yes." Here's your chance to say, "NO!" Throw the guilt out the window; you haven't done anything wrong! Honor yourself.

# Exercise

*Exercise—fuel for the body.*

If you're sitting and can stand, do so now. It's time to begin. Ready? And a five, six, seven, eight!

In order to survive, it's essential to breathe, eat, sleep, and EXERCISE. No, I didn't sneak that last one in just to be mean. Exercise, although not *as* critical to our survival, *is* important.

Whether you like it or not, you're given one body. It may be a body of which you're proud, or a body you'd like to hide. Regardless, it's important to exercise it. As Newton so aptly put it, "Bodies in motion tend to stay in motion." So **MOVE**. Give your body the fuel it requires to stay strong, flexible, and healthy.

I know for some of you the idea of exercising is as attractive as having a root canal, but a few hours a week is all you need to be healthier—mentally and physically. Exercise does not have to be painful (maybe a little), or too time-consuming. Pick an activity that's fun for you. Maybe you like frisbee golfing, or dancing, or going for long hikes. Remember, you're not training for a marathon; you're just moving your body so that it can be strong, agile, and limber. What if you're wheel-chair-bound and are unable to get up to exercise?

Then strengthen your arms, or your fingers, if possible. Work with what you have.

When you exercise, you create energy, build stamina, and build strength. Forget that cup of coffee in the morning. Go for a walk instead, maybe even to the coffee shop for extra motivation. All you need are your legs and the "DDs"—discipline and dedication. Just so you know, walking at three miles per hour for half an hour helps to stimulate your heart and increases your lung capacity.

*Choose not to run out of gas—exercise!*

We have approximately 640 muscles in our bodies. A large percentage of those, if not exercised, will become flabby and weak. When you exercise, you choose a fitter-looking you. What if you're genetically perfect and look as though you exercise when you really don't? Don't be fooled. That's only on the outside. You need to exercise your insides as well, especially your heart. Studies have shown that exercising helps prevent heart disease. When you exercise your heart muscle regularly, you make it stronger.

To start exercising, joining a fancy gym is not necessary. Work with what you have. Don't let yourself be scared off by commercials with "perfect"-looking bodies. Personal trainer Lisa-Michelle Kapp always said, "Exercising is about quality of life; it is not about a flat stomach, or a better butt. Those are just perks, not the goal."

Regular exercise has many other perks:

1) It can slow down the aging process, making you feel and look younger (and it's a lot cheaper than plastic surgery).

2) It can decrease the risk of osteoporosis (thinning of the bones) by strengthening the muscles around the bones.

3) It can decrease the chances of stroke in individuals who suffer from high-blood pressure.

Right about now, you might be thinking, *But I hate to exercise; it hurts, and it makes me sweat. Ew.* It's easy to feel like that if your body is used to sedentary living, and your main form of exercise is getting up to go to the fridge between commercials. But once your body gets a taste of endorphins (produced by the pituitary and hypothalamus glands during exercise), you'll get that feeling known as an "endorphin rush" and a feeling of well-being. That's when you'll get hooked. I know I did.

My husband and I get up at 5:40 a.m. three days a week to go to the gym. When the alarm goes off, there's nothing more I would love to do than to stay in bed, all cozy and warm. But I don't. Instead, I get myself up and dressed with the gym clothes I laid out the night before. My husband is usually about two minutes behind me. I'm yawning all the way to the gym, still thinking about those warm blankets. At the time of this writing, the trip to the gym was especially hard because we were on a **30-**

**Day Full Body KILLER Workout**. Talk about pain. It was hard getting started, but guess what? By the end of the workout, we felt GREAT! It was like being high on drugs. We were both filled with energy and in upbeat moods, our bodies happy and our minds alert. I don't suggest you start a "Killer" workout, just any workout! It's all good, as long as you're moving.

As you can see, there are a lot of physical benefits to exercising. But that's not all. Exercising also helps to relieve stress. When you're stressed out and anxious, your body releases a hormone called adrenaline. This adrenaline increases your heart rate, blood pressure, and blood glucose. This can cause insomnia, nervousness, and a lowered immune system. But relax. There's something you can do. Exercise! It helps to reduce the amount of adrenaline released during times of high duress. Next time you feel stressed out, try walking, swimming, t'ai chi, bicycling, cleaning your house, or gardening. Any, or all, of those will do. Exercise *can* be fun.

Before you start exercising, it's a good idea to consult your doctor. Once you have the go-ahead, go ahead!

"Exercise can be regarded as tribute to the heart."

~Gene Tunney

# CHOOSE to EXERCISE.

*\*\*\**

## *EXERCISE*

1) Yoga. The great stretches will get you in shape in no time.

2) Dance to your favorite music, maybe some oldies but goodies; I guarantee you'll be smiling and reminiscing before you know it.

3) Take a walk in the park. Breathe in the oxygen from the trees.

4) Take up gardening. The results? Amazing flowers and plants.

5) Wash your car. Believe it or not, that works most of your body. And you'll have a clean car in the process.

6) Golfing. You can burn up to 700 calories or more, depending on the number of holes and whether you're carrying your clubs around.

7) Start moving. That's it. Just start moving.

# Forgive

*Forgiveness—the purifier for your soul.*

Imagine you're carrying a backpack filled with years of *HURT* and *WRONGDOING*, done to you and by you, each weighing several pounds. Depending on your age and how much you've collected, the bag may weigh a little or a lot. Whatever the weight, chances are you feel weighed down and will certainly feel better by emptying the bag completely. Choose to lighten your load. How? By forgiving yourself and those who've hurt you. To forgive is to gain peace of mind, to walk with a lighter step.

What does it mean to forgive? It means to let go, to give up the pain that, if nurtured, breeds uncontrollably, like weeds in a field. Before any healing can take place, forgiveness *has* to occur. Let's take a look at the true story below and see how a hurtful situation evolves:

*Thirty-four-year-old "Mark" calls his father the night before he and his family are to move. He doesn't leave a message, just hangs up. His father "Tom" doesn't see the missed call until the following day. Since there was no message, Tom doesn't worry about it and goes to work like he normally does on Saturdays. Unbeknownst to Tom, Mark feels hurt and disappointed that his father didn't call back. What Mark wanted was to borrow his dad's truck for the move. Tom had no idea that his son and family were even moving or he'd have made arrangements. Mark feels neglected and abandoned and stops talking to his father. Months later the silent treatment continues. Family events are awkward and uncomfortable. Mark is aloof and barely looks at Tom. The family now has a big crack down the middle, not unlike the San Andreas Fault. Mark's perceived injury?—his father "abandoned" him when he needed him. Two years later, his emotions have become too big to manage. He still hasn't talked to his father.*

As an outsider, you can probably see the ridiculousness of the situation. But for Mark, it is very real and painful. Families and friendships break up all the time for things this trite and even less so. Have you experienced a similar situation in your life? Let's take a look at what Mark could have done differently and still kept his family intact. Mark could have asked himself, "What am I really upset about? Am I upset because my father didn't help me out? I actually didn't give him any notice." Or "Am I upset because he didn't call me back? I could have left a message." Understanding the real reason for the upset might just make things more clear, and he'd be able to see that no harm had actually been intended. Anything that isn't addressed is stored in the heart and becomes even more painful over time.

Mark could have saved himself a lot of hurtful emotions by saying, "Hey, Dad, what happened yesterday? I was hoping to borrow your truck! Why didn't you call me back?" He would have heard his father's side of the story and understood that there was no intentional malfeasance. The situation could have been resolved right then and there.

To this day, Mark continues to hold onto the perceived "terrible" thing his father did. Mark will not feel peace until he is able to forgive his father. Even though it's clear that Tom did nothing wrong, in Mark's mind he did.

Unless Mark chooses to talk to his father and forgive him, the situation will not change. That hurt will remain in Mark's heart forever.

When you choose to hold onto whatever grievance was done to you, like Mark has, you give it energy, thereby prolonging the damage long after the original hurtful event. Often the event is replayed repeatedly in your mind's eye, each time causing you more and more emotional pain. It's like constantly picking at a scab and never allowing it to heal. Holding on only keeps you feeling angry and resentful.

What, then, is the solution? To forgive—an act of self-love. Through forgiveness, you give yourself a gift. Instead of feeling resentment, hatred, and vengeance, you feel *PEACE*. In peace, love is all there is. I am reminded of the words of Mark Twain, "Forgiveness is the fragrance that the violet sheds on the heel that has crushed it."

When you forgive, you take your power back. You are no longer the victim. You are a decision-maker. There is great power in choosing forgiveness. Choose to forgive!

*Not forgiving is like having your heart catch fire and doing nothing to put out the flames.*

Forgiving may seem difficult, but it can be quite simple. All you have to do is be willing. Be open. You may no longer want the person who hurt you in your life; that's your choice, of course. However, you can still forgive. All you have to say is, "I forgive you, _____." If, after careful consideration, you decide you don't want to associate with that person, simply say it to yourself. Then let it go. You may want to write the person a letter expressing how you feel, and then another letter having them say what you'd like to hear. When you're done, get rid of the letters. Let them go, along with your hurt and pain. Then live your life, free of resentment and all those negative feelings that come from holding onto the pain. If you feel you need outside help, talk to a therapist, a minister, or a good unbiased friend.

You might think that to forgive is to admit that the other person is right, or that you condone what has taken place. It does not. Forgiving is about releasing *you* from the pain so that you can be free and at peace. Mark has to work at being angry, at remaining aloof, at ignoring his father. How much better would he feel if he just let go and forgave his father? His heart would be able to expand with love and understanding.

Forgiveness does not only mean forgiving others for their wrongdoings, it also means forgiving yourself. Forgiving yourself is often just as difficult as forgiving someone else. Sometimes even more so.

Maybe there's something you did that has bothered you for years, kept preserved in a special place in your being—always there causing you pain when you least expect it. There is nothing that can be done about the past. Don't condemn yourself to a lifelong sentence. Simply learn from your experience and move forward.

Forgiveness is a great healer. Heal thyself. You can choose to do so. Choose to forgive, thereby creating a new life with more joy and happiness.

"If you want to see brave, look at those who can forgive."

~Bhagavad Gita

# CHOOSE to FORGIVE!

\*\*\*

## *EXERCISE*

1) Think of one person toward whom you have ill feelings. Then say, "I forgive [insert name of person here] for [insert grievance here]. I let go of the resentment. I am free." Repeat this like a mantra. Anything you say to yourself, your brain believes. Brain research shows that the brain is capable of creating long-term memory. If you rehearse, talk, or imagine something for at least 18 seconds, it gets stored in your long-term memory bank. Imagine now what great things you could store in there!

2) Think of something you wish you'd never done, for which you feel guilty. Then say, "I forgive myself. I no longer harbor ill feelings. I live in peace."

Say the words above every day, or as long as you need to, in order to feel a sense of calmness in your life. You may not believe them at first. Act as if you do. Eventually the good feelings will take over. Let them.

# Give

*When you give, you receive with interest.*

Do you want to feel good? Do you want to get that warm and fuzzy feeling inside? It's simple ... GIVE. That's what giving is all about—feeling good—both for the giver and the receiver. Ideally, giving is best when done unconditionally. Giving with strings attached loses its magic, its sincerity.

When you give, you activate the Law of Circulation, which is basically the law of giving and receiving. All things in the universe are always flowing and circulating. There are no limits. In fact, it's always expanding. When you give, you receive. One does not exist without the other. Imagine giving to be the same as jumping. You can't jump up without coming back down. It's the same with giving. You can't give without receiving. Think of it as universal gravity.

I am not encouraging you to give with the idea of getting something back; the minute you do, giving becomes conditional. Anything you give with an "expectation tag" attached is a bribe. It's like saying, "I gave you a 'just-because' card. Isn't that sweet? What will you give me in return?" Without realizing it, you might be looking to get stroked for your kindness. "Wow, Katie, you're so thoughtful!" Even expecting a "thank you" in this example is placing a condition on the action. I've heard people say irately, "I can't believe it! I gave Mike a ride, and he didn't even thank me." While saying "thank you" is a polite thing to do, don't upset yourself if you don't get it. Give without anticipating a return on your investment. It is our expectations that usually lead to disappointments. With unconditional giving, there is no room for hard feelings, only room for the feeling of pure love, joy, and acceptance.

*You don't have to give big, just give what you can.*

One of the things you can bank on getting back when you give willingly and unconditionally is an incredible feeling of deep joy. You might be thinking, *I don't have anything to give. I don't have much money.* I'm not just talking about giving things that require money. Although, if you have it and want to share it, that's great. I am talking about giving what you do have. How about the gift of a smile? What a joy it is to see someone smile. Try it next time you're out and about. The person at whom you smile will feel validated, acknowledged. A smile, as insignificant as you might think it is, may be just what someone needs to receive at that moment.

How about a text or a phone call just to say "hi"? A couple of years ago, I was getting into my car when I noticed I had a missed call. I was tired and out of energy. When I listened to my voicemail, I heard the voice of my then two-year-old granddaughter saying "hi" and "I love you" in her cute, little voice. Of course, she didn't actually make the call; she had a little help, but that simple message made my whole day. I immediately called her nanny back to thank her for such a precious gift.

How about giving of your time? Ralph Waldo Emerson said, "The only gift is a portion of yourself." You are valuable by virtue of being you. Can you think of anyone who would like to spend time with you? It could just be 15 minutes listening to someone talk about their day, their dreams, their children, their favorite show, anything.

My parents are both in their mid 80s. They live with my husband and me and have pretty much the same routine every day. I make it a point to spend 20-30 minutes in the mornings with them while I eat my breakfast. They eagerly wait for me to share anything new that is happening in my life. We watch the news and talk about the siblings or anything else that happens to be going on at the time. Sometimes I feel rushed and would prefer to not sit there for that short period of time, and then I think, *What's 20 minutes in the grand scheme of things? You can afford to take time from your busy schedule to chat for a few minutes with people who look forward to having your company.* Time is a great gift. Think about a person in your life who would like more of yours.

How about giving away authentic, sincere compliments? Think back to the last time you were paid a compliment ... how did it make you feel? Did you think about it for some time afterward? I have a hunch you probably did. Late one night, I received a text from a good friend. She'd texted,

"Do you know that your inner peace and delight shine through? You sparkle." I fell asleep feeling good and happy, a smile on my face. Both giving and receiving feel great in the heart.

I was once coming out of the bank and noticed a woman with a really cute haircut. I stopped and let her know how good the cut looked on her. She was gushing. "Really?" she said. "I just cut it yesterday and wasn't sure if I'd made the right choice." I could see I'd made her day with that simple compliment. It was easy and priceless at the same time. And it made me feel splendid to see her face light up.

When you give, you get back twice as much. Receive it. Keep some. Give the rest away. Give a hand; yours may be the only one around. Give your kindness away. If you don't get it back immediately, that's okay. Someone else will give you theirs when you least expect it, maybe when you need it most. Give freely.

"Giving is the master key to success in all applications of human life."

~Bryant McGill

# CHOOSE to GIVE. Its power is magnificent.

## *EXERCISE*

Today, find a way to give, however small the giving may seem.

1) Send a card to someone who's not expecting it. Do it in the old-fashioned way. Actually buy a card, fill it out, and mail it. Don't you love getting mail?

2) Give a hand to someone who needs it. Is there someone you know who might benefit from a little help from you? Think of the difference you might be able to make.

3) Text someone and let them know you love them. Or just send a little smiley face to let them know you're thinking about them.

4) Spend time with someone who might be missing you. Is there someone you haven't seen in a while? Perhaps it's time to reconnect. Think about it. They might be thinking about you.

# Honor

*When you honor yourself, you express self-love.*

Working hard at school could get you on the *HONOR* roll. Working even harder might result in you graduating with *HONORS*. Fighting for your country might earn you the highest military award—the Medal of *HONOR*. And traveling might get you to the Point of *HONOR* Museum in Lynchburg, Virginia.

Receiving honors and visiting architectural landmarks are all well and good, but none equal the greatest form of honor: HONORING YOURSELF. To honor yourself means to respect who you are; to appreciate your value—in relation to your family, your community, the universe, and most importantly, yourself. Honoring who you are means recognizing your importance, not discounting or minimizing yourself in any way.

I met a young woman several months back who was having trouble honoring herself. In fact, she despised who she was. She felt *less than* most people, and she constantly criticized herself for existing. Despite her feelings, she wanted to meet a man with whom she could have a relationship. I explained that in order for her to meet a man who would love and honor her, she had to start loving and honoring herself. If not, why would anyone else want to? She had a long road ahead of her, but after our conversation, she understood that she deserved to be here and that she was lovable, no matter what anyone else might say to her.

Many of you find it easy to idolize others—to put movie stars, musicians, sports figures, and the like, up on pedestals. In the meantime, you continuously criticize and judge yourself, like the young woman in the example above. To love yourself seems to be an ongoing battle. While it is okay to respect the work of other people, and to enjoy their talents and contributions, it is not okay to feel you are inferior because you are not a movie star, a musician, or a sports figure.

Imagine your Earth as a bird sanctuary. Now imagine yourself as one of the birds—a cardinal, a finch, a mockingbird, etc. Birds in the sanctuary sing their special song; not one bird is considered less adequate than any of the other birds. The birds don't judge or criticize themselves for singing off-key, or for being a different color or size. You're not going to hear, "Hey, look at that Rufous Whistler over there on that branch. His whistling sounds a bit off. And what about that Blue Jay? Geesh, that blue is just a tad too boring. And don't even get me started on that Yellow Oriole. That yellow is so bright, it's making me blind." What the birds do is create a beautiful medley that fills the sanctuary with an awesome melody. Each bird is unique, its song unequaled.

The parallel is obvious. You are a unique and irreplaceable member of our Earth sanctuary. No one can take your place. So honor yourself. Do and say things that create warm and loving feelings in you. Focus on your uniqueness and the positive aspects of who you are. Then embrace that which makes you YOU! People will treat you how you treat yourself. If you want respect, respect yourself. If you want friends, be one. If you want to be loved, love others. When you do, everything else falls into place.

*Embrace your perfection.*
*Honor every beat of your heart,*
*every breath you take.*

At this point, I would like to offer you a License of Honor. It reads as follows:

*I, _____, honor who I am. I am unique, special, and irreplaceable. I am entitled to daily doses of love and kindness, given to me, by me. I do not judge, criticize, or belittle myself, nor do I need to point out my flaws. Instead, I focus on my inner beauty, my strength, my talents, and my contributions. I work on becoming the best I can be. Daily!*

Any violation of this license will mean serving on the Honor Committee, where you are mandated to work every day—at home, at work, wherever you are—on honoring the person you are. This may seem like a monumental task. For those of you who don't feel good about yourselves, this may even seem like an impossible request to fill. Like any new undertaking, baby steps are required when first starting out.

Honor yourself and take your place proudly in your Earth sanctuary. There's no other place like it, no other person like you. You have been given wings. Know that you can fly anywhere, anytime. Spread your wings and soar. When you do, you will find Heaven on Earth.

"Honor the space between no longer and not yet."

~Nancy Levin

# CHOOSE to HONOR yourself!

\*\*\*

### *EXERCISE*

Like a flower that needs to be watered for it to grow and bloom, you need to honor yourself so that you can become the best you can be. Water yourself with kindness.

1) **Honor Your Mind**: Read, learn something new, and ask a lot of questions.

2) **Honor Your Body**: Exercise it, eat & sleep well, and take time to relax.

3) **Honor Your Heart**: Have self-respect, be kind to yourself, and think positive thoughts.

# Improve

*Cease to improve and you cease to grow.*

You are a work in progress. That means that for as long as you're here on Earth, you get to work on yourself and find ways to become an even better you. That doesn't take away from how wonderful you already are at this moment. But as a work in progress, your work is never done. Imagine you're a house. Sometimes there's clutter that needs to be cleared, or dust that needs to be wiped away, or maybe too much noise from a nearby neighbor. The work in a home is never done, and neither is it done with you.

Every day you are given a gift, a new opportunity to improve yourself and to help others do the same thing. What you choose to do today determines who you will be tomorrow. You can reinvent yourself at any given time. My dear friend Martha has a 12-year-old son who is requiring less and less of her time. Despite the fact that she's in her 40s, she has decided to reinvent herself and will soon be starting law school. If you are not happy with who you are, change your mind. You are not stuck! Don't ever let the phrase, "I've always been this way," prevent you from changing something with which you're not 100% happy.

Take some time now to think about the different areas of your life that could be better, areas where you feel you're lacking: you, your home, your work, your relationships, etc. Examine each of those areas carefully. As a matter of fact, jot each of those down; then underneath, write where you are now and where you'd like to see yourself in the future. What are you willing to do to make an improvement? Let's start with you.

What can you improve? Physically, are you in the best shape possible? Do you feel strong, flexible? Are you energetic? If not, then here's an area on which to work. Mentally, are you stimulating your mind enough? Have you explored any new ideas lately? Have you read any interesting books? Incorporated a new word into your vocabulary? Or do you just vegetate in front of your 50" screen TV mindlessly watching show after show? Maybe spending hours binge-watching *Stranger Things*? Now that's a cozy idea … Watching TV is not bad, in and of itself; it's finding a balance between that and other things.

How is your attitude? Do you let stress dictate your mood? If so, you may need a little tune-up. Your car needs regular checkups and oil changes every few thousand miles, right? You do, too! (Not oil changes, of course, but little tune-ups here and there.) Personal adjustments can be made at all times. Maybe you want to change up your wardrobe or your hairstyle. I used to have a friend who'd worn the same hairstyle since she was a teen. Almost always wore the same color, tan. She lacked the confidence to make even slight personal changes.

Perhaps you want to start taking steps to get fit. Or maybe you want to work on controlling your anger, or getting rid of a bad habit. Don't wait for every 3,000 miles, hours, days, or months. Do it now!

How about your inner world? Do you take time to quiet yourself? To get in touch with that inner center that often holds key answers for your life— answers that may help you with your daily blocks and hurdles? Let yourself be guided by that intuitive part of you that has your best interest at heart.

What about your home? Check it out. What might you be able to improve there? Are you surrounded by clutter? Every corner and tabletop filled with something? How about doing some reorganizing, taking time to de-clutter and get rid of stuff you don't even remember is there? You'll feel lighter, feel freer, and have an overall sense of wellness. The time of the year doesn't matter. I just recently went through my closet. There were quite a few pretty dresses and shirts that I never wore. In the past, I'd get sentimental and think about how much I liked them. This time I thought, *If I like them so much, why don't I ever wear them*? Then I threw them in the bag and donated them. Didn't blink an eye. I liberated my closet from items that were no longer useful in my life.

When was the last time you rearranged your furniture? The results can be refreshing. Maybe your phone greeting needs a little energy boost. Try something new. I'm not suggesting you make big improvements, just little bits here and there.

What about your workplace? What needs a little renovation there? Examine your work area. Can you find what you need when you need it? If you can't, take some time to make some sense out of the mess. Get organized.

How are your relationships? They are one of the most important things you can improve. They are your support system, your refuge when you need it. They are the people who know you best and would be the first to help you. Look for ways to improve all of them, especially those with family and friends. Send someone a letter letting them know they're in your thoughts. I know e-mails and texts are quick and easy, but I always find it exciting to receive a handwritten letter or card in the mail. Surprise a friend with whom you haven't spoken in a while; give him or her a call. Invite a loved one out to lunch. Pick up the check. Show appreciation for the things people do. Giving and gratitude are amazing healers. They create self-confidence, joy, and happiness.

Improvement is a choice away. Make that choice. Changes don't have to be monumental or life-altering. Explore all the possibilities. Start today!

"To improve is to change; to be perfect is to change often."

~Winston Churchill

# CHOOSE to IMPROVE.

## *EXERCISE*

This week, choose to improve one thing in your life:

1) Your knowledge
2) Your attitude
3) Your surroundings
4) Your relationships
5) Your appearance

# Jog

*Jog yourself awake. Welcome to your life!*

Before you panic and think this chapter is about jogging four miles a day, relax. This chapter has nothing to do with exercise. At least not the physical kind. This will be a mental exercise—an exercise that can add color and zest to your life if only you would rouse yourself to alertness.

For many of you, life has become a conditioned response—a repetitive dance without the excitement of a new step. Life has become a predictable routine that begins and ends the same way, just like in the movie *Groundhog Day*. In that film, Bill Murray's character, Phil, a cynical weatherman, was forced to relive every single day in the same manner until he learned whatever lessons were needed to become a better person. There was no variance. In real life, however, if you go through life doing the same things over and over again, that's it! One day it will be over. You're not just going to wake up and get another chance to make different choices.

It is easy to cruise and live life as if by rote: up at the same time, same route to work and back, same flavored coffee, same conversations with coworkers, same music station, same hostility in rush hour traffic, etc. Why? Fear to step out of the comfort zone—the box you've created for yourself.

This fear creates a numbness you may not even realize exists because it has become a way of life. Wake up! It's time to set the alarm and jog yourself out of your slumber. You'll be amazed at how alive you'll feel. And isn't that what you want? Once you wake up, you won't want to go back to sleep.

Take a look at your life. By this I mean, examine what you do on a daily basis from the moment you wake up in the morning until you retire for the night. It might be interesting to keep a journal for a week and check out what it is you do, and how much time you spend doing it.

Are you taking your life for granted? Do you go through daily robotic motions? Motions that do nothing but get you from one moment to the next in the same exact way as the day before? Does the schedule in your daily planner or smartphone look the same day after day?

I'm not saying that planning and having some rituals and routines is a bad thing. They are, in fact, necessary. It's important to get to work or school every day. It is important to eat, to have friends, etc. What I'm saying is that a variation to the daily routine is essential to let us know we're alive and kicking. It's good to shake things up a bit; change the design of your life.

Imagine going to a concert and the music having no key changes, no accents, and no crescendos— just one long, indistinguishable melody that sounds exactly the same throughout. Would you want to listen? How enjoyable would it be? Does your life have key changes? Accents? Crescendos?

If you can't think of any offhand, then it's time to **JOG** yourself into action, into changing up your daily, predictable patterns.

You might be saying, "But I'm happy with my life!" That's great. This is not about being unhappy with your life. It's about being too comfortable. It's scary to try new things. After all, you won't know what to expect. But that's part of the excitement. You'll learn new things, you'll meet different people, and you'll stimulate your mind. The rewards are many. What if you were to play chess and the outcome was the same each time? What would be the incentive to play again? After all, you'd already know that your knight would be captured, that you'd lose your queen, and that you'd inevitably hear the fateful words, "Check-mate!" Chess is exciting because it's unpredictable. The game ends differently each time you play. Yes, when you play chess, you *can* anticipate that you will lose some of your pieces, but you don't know which ones or how many. You can anticipate that the game will last a while, but you don't know how long. And the anticipation of victory is just a move away. Play your life the same way. Anticipate what you must, and let life swirl you around in its amazing vastness.

Jog yourself awake! Life is more than the box you have built for yourself. Cut the box open. Step out! Breathe in the excitement of a new and interesting journey. Put the fear aside and enjoy the refreshing newness. Go ahead and make plans, but be flexible. Flexibility allows new experiences to enter into your life. Without those new experiences, your lives will become repetitive and monotonous. Make every moment count while you're here.

"Jog your way into action and let the momentum take you further than you've ever been."

~Rossana Snee

# CHOOSE to JOG yourself into life!

\*\*\*

## *EXERCISE*

Wake up. Ease yourself out of hibernation. Try:

1) A new language. You can do this in your car on your way to work.

2) A new pair of eyeglasses. There are so many amazing styles out there.

3) A different hairstyle. Start looking at different pictures. What strikes your fancy?

4) A different morning cereal.

5) A different radio station. Try listening to AM radio, or Spanish or country music.

6) A different genre of book. Don't get sucked into the same thing every time you read.

# Know

*Surrender and allow yourself to know.*

It's time to talk about:

1) What you know, and ...

2) What you think you know.

There are certain things you *do* know. It's safe to say that you know your name, your date of birth, your address, and your telephone number. Oh, and that you have to pay taxes! It's also safe to say you know who most of your immediate family members are, including their names, where they live, and most of their birthdays. I am sure there are many more things that could be added to the list of things you know for sure. Then there are the things you think you know.

Most of you *think* you know what you're going to do in the next half hour, the following week, or even a year from now. You *think* you'll get home at a certain time, or that you're going to get home at all. You *think* you'll be married for the rest of your life to the same person, or that you'll live in the same home until you die. The truth of it is that all of these things are unknown. Unexpected calls, natural disasters, divorces, and foreclosures say otherwise. In actuality you really don't know. Outside of the precise moment in which you exist, you don't know a whole lot; you just *think* you do.

Thirty-seven-year-old Sebastien Bellin, a former Brazilian-Belgian basketball player, thought that it would be travel as usual on March 22, 2016. An explosion at the airport in Brussels, Belgium, however, caused by the terrorist group *Islamic State of Iraq & the Levant* (ISIL), changed all that. Miraculously, Sebastien survived. Sebastien didn't know that his travel day would become a historic event leaving him injured, wheelchair-bound, and guilt-ridden. What Sebastien now knows is that he could never have predicted any of it.

Knowing that this is the only moment in which you exist can change your entire life. How? One, you can stop worrying about the **PAST** you know existed but no longer does. It is history and cannot be altered. Generally, you use the past to torment yourself about things you should or shouldn't have done. Two, you can stop worrying about a **FUTURE** that does not yet exist—a future that in no way, shape, or form you can predict, no matter how hard you try or want to. So, you're left with **NOW**. This precise moment. Without the worry of the past or future, you are free to concentrate on what you *do* know: This Moment!

*Know you have a purpose. Discover it!*

You may be wondering what there is to know about this moment. Or you may be thinking this moment is just like any other moment. Know that no two moments are alike. Ever! Know that every moment leads you to the next. Every moment creates your life. What kind of life do you want?

Know that no moment should be discarded as unimportant or trivial. There is a breath in each of those moments. How important is that breath? A matter of life or death. Each moment is priceless, to be treasured and savored like a fine meal, a peaceful night's sleep, a hug from a child, support from a friend, or love from a spouse. Know that each moment is a gift. All you have to do is unwrap it. How do you do that? Easy ... KNOW that you're in the moment. Be nowhere else. Always be mindful of where you are, with whom, and of what you're doing; in that way, you remain present.

*Know you are an expression of what you believe about yourself. Believe the best!*

Know that you are here for a special reason, your *Soul* Purpose, if you will. You are here to express yourself and live out your dream, if only you would reach for it. You are here to experience every aspect of life. Imagine your world as a giant supermarket, **DreaM'art**. Each "specially-marked" item is someone's dream. One of them is yours. Decide what you want, and throw it into your life cart. The item will not, on its own, fall into it. You have to grab it, make the trip to the checkout stand, wait in line, and then pay for it.

Some of you may think you *know* that your life is not important. Know that you're wrong! Absolutely wrong! Your life's worth cannot be measured. Know there is no other life like it. Growing up, you may have heard false messages telling you that you were not good enough—

maybe you were even blamed for being born—and you grew up believing those lies. It's time to discard them, to change the tape in your head. Know that whoever fed you those lies didn't know any better. Perhaps they themselves were fed a similar diet of lies growing up.

Know that you are remarkable. Once you realize this, act accordingly. Your life is too precious to be lived out on the sidelines, in the past, or in the future. Know there is one YOU. Share it with the world. Be in each moment fully. Be a star in whatever capacity you can. Remember ... you can!

"You are very powerful, provided you know how powerful you are."

~Yogi Bhajan

# CHOOSE to K*NOW*!

\*\*\*

## *EXERCISE*

Today, take time to know certain truths about yourself:

1) ***Know*** you have unlimited potential.

2) ***Know*** you have the power to change your life.

3) ***Know*** you can make a difference.

4) ***Know*** you are responsible for your actions.

# Learn

*Learn. It feeds your mind.*

Listen up, students … **SCHOOL IS IN SESSION!** You have an incredible opportunity to learn as much as you desire. All you have to do is choose to do so.

Generally you have no problem feeding your body. Food tends to be a top priority for the majority of people. Most celebrations usually revolve around food. TV commercials show beautiful people dripping sauce on their nice clothes, and they don't care. Why? Because they're eating something delicious. People like to be fed.

There's something else that needs to be fed: your mind. It needs to learn. Mahatma Gandhi put it quite nicely when he said, "Live as if you were to die tomorrow. Learn as if you were to live forever." When you choose to learn, you exercise your mind; you put an end to intellectual blindness.

Learning is the fuel that keeps your mind alive and alert. Learning is the opportunity to move to higher levels, to leave behind your ignorance. You might be asking, "What should I learn?" The answer is: **EVERYTHING YOU CAN**! Nothing is out of bounds. Everywhere you look, a learning opportunity exists.

Learning can be fun. You can learn something by yourself and share it. Or, you can learn something with a friend and share it. Make a list of all the things you want to learn. When you're done, make another list. Then another.

*Learning creates a brighter life. Brighten your life!*

I had the privilege of meeting a woman by the name of Joanne Noar. She started taking figure skating lessons at the ripe age of 65. At the time of this writing, she was 72. She told me she was always learning something physically and mentally. "It's good to have a balance," she said. Joanne was studying particle physics and astronomy. She would listen to audiotapes on the way to the rink, and she would play the piano half an hour every day. She considered learning a gift. She said, "There is so much to learn. It's so exciting. You *can* teach an old dog new tricks. Learning makes life fun." Her philosophy was, "If someone else can do it, I can do it, too! There is always something fun waiting for you."

When I was 52, I accompanied a good friend to an art supply store. It felt like being in a candy store even though I didn't know the first thing about painting. I told my friend how much I wished I were an artist like my dad. She said, "You're already an artist. I can tell by all the pictures of paintings you have on your phone." That comment took me by surprise. Right then I made a decision to learn how to paint. When I got home, I asked my dad if he'd teach me how to paint with acrylics. At first my work looked like that of a kindergartner's. But in a few short months, I started to make amazing progress. Much to my delight, I really did become an artist. Painting has become one of my passions. It took one little comment to fuel the fire that had been burning within me.

Clearly, learning is not only for the young. Many people, as they get older—whatever older means to them—start slowing down. I often hear 40-year-olds say, "I'm getting too old for this," or, "My body doesn't move like it used to." If you believe you're slowing down, you are. The good news is that if you keep learning, your mind will continue to be fed. The universe gives you what you want, what you believe you deserve. So, if you have limiting beliefs, change your beliefs! You are never too old. Age is a limitation only if you let it be. Don't let it.

*The only walls blocking your learning are built by you. Tear down the walls.*

What does it take to learn? Making a choice and putting in the effort. You can choose to learn a multitude of things. Perhaps you want to learn how to dance, rock climb, hike, or ski. But that's not enough; it would be like only taking P.E. in school. You won't be able to get enough credits. There are many other things to learn. How about painting, sculpting, or playing an instrument? How about learning new communication skills, or how to speak in public? How about learning to cook, to garden, or to perform CPR? How about learning how to be more patient, tolerant, and nonjudgmental? We are all in the same school, just at different grade levels. Others may not be as advanced as you, or they may be more so. Learn to get along. Allow the more advanced to be mentors; tutor the ones just starting out.

*Knowledge is power. Choose to be powerful!*

Make every day about learning something. You'll never run out of material. Whatever you choose to do in your life, make it a learning experience, and then enjoy the benefits. Our Earth is a school—be its student. Choose to learn until the day you graduate.

"You learn something every day if you pay attention."

~Ray LeBlond

# CHOOSE to LEARN.

\*\*\*

## *EXERCISE*

This week, begin to learn something new. Choose anything at all as long as you're learning. How about:

1) Another language

2) Something you don't know about someone you love

3) Another culture

4) Another religion

5) Another part of the country

6) A new way to do something you already know

# Meditate

*Meditation is a soothing balm for the soul.*

Shhh ... allow your eyes to gently close. Inhale. Take your time. Release it slowly. Feel yourself starting to relax.

*"RELAX?! I can't do that. I have too much to do!"* you say.

From the moment you wake up, you're on full speed ahead. You go, go, go! Is it any wonder, then, that there's so much stress? Nearly everyone seems to feel overwhelmed and be suffering from varying degrees of anxiety. In a world full of distractions, constant movement, and unending frenzy, there seems to be little time to be still.

There appears to be more concern with what's going on in the external world than with what's happening in the internal one. You spend a major portion of your time working, checking Facebook or any other social media, shopping, running errands, etc. How much time do you actually spend going within? For many of you, it's no time at all. You're lost in the rat race. In order to have balance in your life, it is important to feel tranquil and at peace. Meditation is key—it stills the mind and awakens your soul. Let yourself be guided. Hear the voice within.

Meditation has been considered a way to deepen the state of understanding and is thought to have healing powers. As a matter of fact, the Latin root for the word meditation ("mederi") means "to heal." Meditation has been used as a way to heal the mind and body. It can actually create structural changes to the brain. It can also help generate new circuits by altering the way in which the neurons communicate with each other. So if you have a negative mindset, for example, meditation might aid in changing the course of your thought patterns, making them more positive. Your body will also feel its effects. You can reduce the risk of heart disease, improve your immune system, and even lower your blood pressure.

Through meditation you can:

1) Quiet your mind's constant chatter.

2) Learn to focus; be in the moment.

3) Feel more in harmony, physically and spiritually.

4) Reduce stress.

Meditation practices, like tiger stripes, are unique to each individual. Meditation doesn't have to take long. A few minutes a day is all you need to get started. Don't worry if you find meditation difficult at first. Be patient. You may want to try different approaches until you find the way that feels best for you. For now, let's try this:

1) Sit or lie in a comfortable place, free of distractions. 2) Close your eyes. 3) Relax. One way to do this is to tighten each body part, then release.

You can start with your toes, and then move up to the rest of the body, slowly. 4) Focus on your breathing. Have your breath originate in the lower abdomen. Do this until you start feeling relaxed. 5) Breathe in (mentally count to eight as you do so). Hold your breath for a count of two. Release the breath using a count of 10 (it usually takes longer to exhale completely than to inhale). Repeat this process several times. Keep concentrating on your breathing. If you find yourself thinking about your favorite TV sitcom, it's okay. Acknowledge the thought and refocus on your breathing. When you're ready to stop, open your eyes and allow yourself a minute to leave the meditation. Build up to longer periods.

Some people like to use mantras—a sound, word, or phrase that is repeated throughout the meditation. Your mantra can be spoken aloud, or it can be silent, as long as your focus is on it. For example, you may want to use the word *OM*— which is considered to be the most sacred sound and greatest mantra. The *OM* sound is said to embody the essence of the entire universe. You can also say the phrase, *I AM AT PEACE*. Or, you may even come up with your own. That's one of the beauties of meditation—it can be customized by you, for you!

Here's another suggestion for meditation: After you're relaxed, start counting (silently) from 20 backward. Focus on each number. If you get to 16 and find your mind wandering, make a note of the message you got, if any, and start counting again. Yes, from 20, until you can get all the way to zero without losing your concentration. This will help you learn to focus.

You don't need to spend hours meditating to feel results. With a few minutes a day, you will start to feel refreshed, energized, and more in tune with your inner voice. Discover inner vision through meditation. Let that vision grow wings and carry you peacefully down your path. And as the late Dr. Wayne W. Dyer said so beautifully, "Embrace silence since meditation is the only way to truly come to know your Source."

"Meditation is the bridge between body and soul."

~Rossana Snee

# CHOOSE to MEDITATE.

\*\*\*

## EXERCISE

Pick one day this week to start meditating. Choose any five minutes of that day and quiet yourself. Go within. Shhh! Listen.

# **N**otice

*Notice the details; they create the whole.*

**Rrrrrrrrrrrrring**! Or maybe you hear: ♫ ♪ ♫ ♩♫. Whatever it is, it's time to wake up! It's a new day.

You force yourself out of bed, perhaps after snoozing three or four times, and head for the bathroom with your eyes half shut. Then you inhale your coffee, tea, protein shake, and whatnot, and drive to work, school, or another destination. It might be a short drive or a long commute. So far, what have you noticed? Really noticed?

Many of you are on automatic pilot. You go through the motions and wait for *THE* day. What day, you wonder. The day when something good is going to happen. *That* day. It might be Friday, thank God! Or Wednesday, Hump Day! Or it might be your next vacation day. Or pay day. It might be lunch with that special someone you've been admiring. Don't wait! Today is *THE* day. Notice the wonder around you, the magnificence that is part of your world.

Perhaps you've failed to notice all the special things around you because you're burdened by everyday life. You might be concentrating on your aches and pains, your trouble with your car, or your problematic neighbor. You have become lost in a world of your own making, stuck within the confines of walls you can't see beyond. You are in such a hurry to get to your next stop that you miss the beauty in between. How many of you have seen cars speeding to the stoplight? I see it often, and I wonder, *What's the hurry*? Now they find themselves waiting next to the person they just passed going 20 MPH faster.

Nowadays your BFF is your appointment book, or for most of you, your smartphone. No matter which one, they are filled, brimming with schedules that absorb your whole day. Make an appointment to *NOTICE*.

What can you do? You can *STOP*! That's right. *LISTEN*! The world is full of gifts—gifts for your enjoyment and pleasure. Downshift. Park. Take a good look around you. Did you see the sunrise this morning? Did you hear the chattering birds in the trees? Did you feel that soft breeze on your face? Did you actually stop to smell the roses? As you go through the day, take time to notice those moments and many more. That's what life is—a series of moments. So pay close attention.

A coworker of my husband's was telling him about a motorcycle ride he'd been on. He'd ridden his bike at 155 MPH. He said he couldn't see a thing. Everything was a blur. All he could do was concentrate on keeping his bike steady. How many of you go through life like that? In a blur? Just concentrating on keeping your life steady? There's so much more!

Next time your alarm goes off, hit snooze and *LISTEN*. Don't worry; it's only for a few minutes.

Don't be in too much of a hurry to get up. If necessary, set your alarm to go off five minutes earlier. Can you hear the cars in the distance? The stillness of the early morning? Clinking wind chimes on your porch? A dog barking? An airplane overhead?

*Slow down. Notice everything!*

When you leave your house today, pay close attention to the details you generally ignore. Imagine you've lived a life without sight and hearing. What would your reaction be? Imagine this often.

A while back, I saw a film called *About Time*. The main character could travel back in time just by closing his fists in a dark space. Having that ability gave him the chance to fix mistakes he had made along the way. When his father passed away, he told his son to live every day twice: the first time just like he normally would, experiencing all the stressors of the day, and the second time just to feel the joy and notice everything he'd missed the day before. Wouldn't it be great if you could do that? Well, you might not be able to go back in time, but you certainly can live the day as if it were your second time. Give it a try.

Moments are everywhere, right in front of you. All you have to do is notice them. Remember, also, to take the time to notice what others do for you. Sometimes those things are taken for granted. Stop now and think of someone who is always there for you, unconditionally. Notice it, and let them know how much you appreciate what they do. It could be a neighbor who always brings in your paper when you're on vacation; the person who lets you cut in line because you have fewer items; the friend who picks up the check; or the mom who buys you a pair of cute earrings, just because she loves you.

Take a look around. See what you've missed. Step out of the silence. Hear what you've missed.

"Life is full of beauty. Notice it. Notice the bumblebee, the small child, and the smiling faces. Smell the rain, and feel the wind. Live your life to the fullest potential, and fight for your dreams."

~Ashley Smith

# CHOOSE to NOTICE.

\*\*\*

## *EXERCISE*

1) As you step out of your house today, notice something different.

2) Next time you turn on your radio, really listen to the lyrics of a song you thought you knew.

3) Make an effort to notice something or someone you've taken for granted.

4) Notice your reaction to different things.

5) Pay attention to the different smells around you.

# Open

*Being open is akin to risking.*
*Risking is akin to living.*

Come out, come out, wherever you are. IT'S TIME!
You will need a sharp object for later; a pin will do.
Time for what? For you to come out of your hiding
place, that imaginary bubble that is keeping you
"safe" and comfortable, but also keeping you from
living life to its fullest. The safety of the bubble is
illusory and limiting. It is a false idea keeping you
from all that life has to offer.

Secure in your bubble, you do all the things that
are familiar: shop at the same stores, buy the same
items, frequent the same restaurants, order the
same foods, drive the same streets, listen to the
same music, and talk to only people you know. In
your imagined refuge, you think the "Boogeyman"
will never get you, and that nothing bad will ever
happen to you. Unfortunately, life, "good" or "bad,"
happens anyway.

Change is usually considered a negative thing, yet
change is all there is. Keeping yourself closed to
change keeps you from growing and expanding.
Whenever something new comes along, what is
your first reaction? Do you welcome it? Or do you
resist it? If you are in the first category, you are
experiencing life more completely. If you are in the
latter category, you may already be in a state of

dormancy. Being in a bubble is like being asleep. You're missing out. I'm not suggesting you jump off a bridge attached to a bungee cord to feel that sought-after adrenaline rush, but to simply be open to new possibilities. Life can be an incredible adventure, or it can be nothing at all.

*Step out of the world you've created.*
*Expand it. Create a new one.*

Think about some of the reasons you refuse to venture out of your cozy domain. I would bet on **FEAR**—that nasty four-letter word. Fear is manipulative. Manipulate *it*! Fear is a control freak. Control *it*! Don't be its slave. Fear is always ready to come out and SCARE YOU TO DEATH. **BOO!**

There is good news, however. It's time! Take out that sharp object I mentioned in the beginning of this chapter. Pop your bubble, and walk out. How? By taking a step you've never taken before. Scared? That's okay. The important thing is to not give into it. Now that you're out, be open to new things. Is there something you've wanted to do, but you've been too afraid to do it? Now is the time to try it.

I used to treat a client who suffered from social anxiety. The fear that she would be humiliated, ostracized, and/or laughed at if she went out kept her stuck in the house. Her world was quite small. She assumed that everyone would look at her and sneer. It was an imagined scenario that more than likely would never happen. And even if it did, what she was missing was far greater. She was missing her life. Voluntarily, she had set limits on her world. She had created her own prison; but she also had the key to her own freedom, if only she'd use it. I suggested she start going out—to take a short walk to her car or down the block. She was to do this daily, extending the length of her excursions every few days. The technique worked because it was doable. She couldn't see herself taking a trip to the mall, but she could cope with a stroll down her street.

Another young woman I knew was kept hostage by her FEAR of being attacked by terrorists. She was so scared that she canceled her trip to Europe. I asked her if she was scared to drive, to which she replied that, no, she wasn't. I then explained to her that car crashes kill 400 times more people than international terrorism in developed countries; in 2001, studies have shown, as many people died every 26 days on American roads as in the terrorist bombings of 9/11. I'd rather take my odds flying to Europe.

*Be open to different ideas. Use them.*
*Come up with some of your own.*

Are you closed-minded? Once you make up your mind, do you hold fast to your beliefs? Refuse to listen to anything that doesn't match with what you hold close to your heart? I'm reminded of a quote: *Some minds are like concrete, all mixed up and permanently set* (author unknown). What is your mind like? Stay open. That's what keeps the world moving.

Here's an idea for opening up: When you hear something new, don't automatically reject it. Think about it. Is it possible? You don't know? Find out. Remember, at one point, the notion of the world being round was ludicrous.

Being open is the first step. Take that step. Don't let fear stop you. There is only one way to conquer fear. Feel it, and then do the action anyway. It will get easier each time you do this.

Resisting this section? Still in your bubble? You have a choice: Stay there or venture out. It's field trip time!

"You have to open your mind, take a second look, and consider the possibilities."

~Ann Young

# CHOOSE to be OPEN!

***

## *EXERCISE*

1) Plan a vacation to a place you've never visited.

2) Paint a wall in your house with an accent color that pops.

3) Visit a restaurant that serves food you've never tried.

4) Explore a topic about which you know little or nothing.

# Persevere

*It's perseverance that binds dreams to reality.*

I wouldn't doubt that a lot of you would like to arrive at your destination without taking the drive. It requires a great amount of patience to plow through bumper-to-bumper traffic in order to reach home. It takes even more patience to travel the roadway to your dreams.

What does it take to arrive at your destination? Perseverance—the ability, the will, to continue to do something despite its difficulty. Do *you* have what it takes to persevere? To not give up? If you think you don't, think again. Perseverance is not some DNA code that you either have or don't have. Everyone has it; it just has to be exercised. Perseverance is like a muscle—the more you exercise it, the stronger it gets.

Visualize a goal you'd like to accomplish. Keep it clear in your mind. That goal can be attained. Most people don't achieve their goals—not because they're "unlucky," but because they give up! So how can you practice perseverance? Simple: **DON'T QUIT!** Make that choice. If you are one of those people who start a project full of enthusiasm but lose steam halfway through it, your perseverance muscle needs strengthening. Start practicing with little things. Choose a project, however small, and see it through to completion, no matter what!

It might be something as simple as completing a crossword puzzle, organizing your DVD shelf, or getting pictures from your last vacation from your computer to an album. When you've mastered these, begin tackling bigger tasks, such as finishing a class or kicking the smoking habit. Remember to always keep your goal in mind.

*Perseverance feeds on drive. Become driven.*

Calvin Coolidge said, "Nothing in this world can take the place of persistence. Talent will not; nothing is more common than unsuccessful men of talent. Genius will not; unrewarded genius is almost a proverb. Education will not; the world is full of educated derelicts. Persistence and determination alone are omnipotent."

Success is not determined by luck or heredity; it is determined by persistence. Successful people just don't give up. That is the reason for their success. Most people tend to abandon ship when a storm hits. A few gusts of wind and some dizzying waves, and they want to bail. Only if you stay on the boat will you reach your destination. This doesn't mean you won't get seasick. Realize that in weathering the storm comes your strength. If you are not encountering any storms along the way, then maybe you haven't left the harbor. Set sail and allow yourself to be swept out into the sea of life.

Perhaps you've heard the media say (about someone famous), "She is an overnight success." Think about that—*an overnight success*?! Really? It doesn't happen. What about the years that person worked toward their goal? Worthwhile goals require a great deal of time and preparation. Think about a natural bodybuilder for a minute. Picture every fiber, every muscle; the fine cut in every square inch of their body. How long do you think it took them to look like that? A few weeks, months? Think again. That body was attained after daily visits to the gym and years of hard work.

*Choose to persevere in your pursuits;*
*it's the only way to make them real.*

Author Jonathan Kellerman is quoted as saying that his recipe for success is one part inspiration, one part perspiration. After two decades of writing persistently and completing eight novels, a publisher finally accepted *When the Bough Breaks*. I had the privilege of talking to Mr. Kellerman on the phone one afternoon. I asked him how he'd managed to keep writing after so many rejections. He told me he loved writing and could never see himself giving up. Fortunately for us readers, Kellerman did not give up. Keep in mind that the need for instant gratification can smother out a dream faster than you can blow out a flame.

Failure is due to lack of discipline and perseverance. As long as you keep working on your goal, success is inevitable. When setbacks arise, successful people see it as a temporary inconvenience. They do not seek relief by giving up. They try even harder. Every successful person knows that to persevere is the key to success. Life is in progress. This is not a practice run. Give it the best you got.

> "Take a step closer to your dream. Let persever-ance be your accomplice."
> ~Rossana Snee

# CHOOSE to PERSEVERE.

*** 

## *EXERCISE*

1) Build the perseverance muscle group. Choose a project or goal. Start small. Perhaps you want to get fit. Begin with a short walk. As you build stamina, increase the length of your walks. Force yourself to keep going, especially when it gets hard and you want to stop.

2) Look within. What is your goal in life? What must you do to attain it? Discipline yourself and succeed. Start by writing down what you'd like to accomplish. Then break it down into small, doable chunks, and attack them one at a time. Eventually you'll get there. But only if you persevere.

# **Q**uestion

*Questions are the stairway to knowledge.*
*Climb that stairway.*

Do you have an inquiring mind? Do you want to know everything you possibly can? Are you a seeker, constantly digging deeper? Or do you live life without ever questioning? Without ever wondering, *What else is there?* All the personal and intellectual growth you gain throughout your life begins with a question and the desire to answer it. With each question, you add a new step, one that takes you to newer and higher levels.

Life itself is a giant question mark. Only through questioning do you evolve. Ignorance isn't bliss. Ignorance keeps you down; it imprisons you. The key to freedom lies in questioning. Your mind is like a sponge. Many people are happy to use just a small portion of it. And then there are those who soak up as much as possible. Which are you? Are you content with what you know right now? Would you like to know more? If so, *question*!

Follow the lead of children. They question all the time. Their thirst for knowledge is unquenchable. Next time you're around a child, listen. You might hear: *How do fingernails grow? Can you sit on a cloud? What makes it rain? If you look at the sun, do you go blind? Why did God invent fleas?* The list is endless. They never tire of asking questions. They want to know everything. What happens to you as you get older? You get busier, overwhelmed, and tired. It doesn't seem that important to question anymore. You're getting by, so you become complacent. The sponge gets a little drier.

What happens if you don't at least moisten the sponge from time to time? Eventually it will dry up completely. Every drop of water that you put on that sponge keeps it moist. Do you want your mind to dry up with old information? Or do you want it to soak up as much as possible? The choice is yours. Make sure to always keep that sponge wet!

How do you know when someone is interested in you? They want to know about you by asking questions. Imagine being on a date. What if he or she stared right through you without saying a word? Not such a fun date, is it? In fact, it would be downright creepy. But what if he or she asked numerous questions in an attempt to know you better? For example, they might say, *Tell me about yourself. What are your hobbies? What's your family like? Do you have siblings? What are some of your favorite foods?* Would you be more likely to go out again? I suspect you would.

You can always pick out the people who are interested in life. They are always doing something to enhance it. They don't settle for mediocrity. They are always questioning, *Am I on the right path? If not, what can I do? How can I get what I want?*

Ignite your mind with questions. Open the gates and allow knowledge to flow in. Don't get comfy with what you know. Always strive to know more. THERE IS ALWAYS MORE. Your age doesn't matter. As a matter of fact, the more you learn, the better it is for your mind as you get older. I once knew a couple—both in their late 80s—who proved this point. The husband (89) was always reading scientific journals, learning about black holes, playing golf, and bowling. His wife, on the other hand, spent her days sitting and watching old sitcoms. Whenever I talked to her, it was obvious she was developing dementia. She would constantly repeat herself, telling the same stories over and over again. At 89 she had multiple strokes and died. I'm not saying this is necessarily what will happen; I'm saying it's a risk if you keep your mind stagnant. Her husband is now almost 93 and still reading his journals, golfing, and bowling. If you stop questioning, you stop learning; your mind stands still. Keep your mind active. Question!

*When you question, you open the door to your mind. Never allow it to close.*

Knowledge is power. Knowledge is your source for growth. Do the research, and then use what you learn to move beyond where you are. You might think you know enough. But how do you *know* when enough is enough?

Imagine an artichoke—that thistle-like plant covered with meaty, spiny leaves. Each time you peel back one of the leaves, you get closer to the heart—what most people consider to be the more savory part of the artichoke. You have to go through many leaves before you get to the heart. It is the same with life. In order to get to the good part, you have to peel back the surface. You do that when you question.

You are on a journey. There *is* a reason you're here; question why. Don't be content to simply coast. Questions are like the gears of the mind; without them our lives stay in neutral.

*Cast aside your ignorance. Don't be afraid to question; be afraid not to.*

Question everything. Pay attention to the answers. There are many. Choose the one that makes sense to you. Explore the ones that don't. Empower yourself.

"Questions wake people up. They prompt new ideas. They show people new places, new ways of doing things."

~Michael Marquardt

# CHOOSE to QUESTION.

\*\*\*

## *EXERCISE*

1) Each day, think of one question that will help you grow as a person.

2) Find the answer.

3) Read something that will prompt you to question.

4) Talk to someone who knows more than you do. Ask questions.

# Release

*Only when you release the old
do you make room for the new.*

Spring is in the air. Take out a broom and dustpan. It's time to clean out your life! For those of you who are pack rats, this section may be a bit tough. I am confident, however, that you will succeed. No maid service or heavy equipment is necessary. You will only need a BOX (for later).

You might be wondering what it is you need to clean out of your life. Clutter! Clutter of which you may be totally unaware. Once you recognize what the clutter is and release it, you will have all the room you need to live out a life filled with joy, peace, happiness, and LOVE.

It's time to take inventory—to take a look at what it is that has been taking up valuable space in your life, leaving you confused, hurt, depressed, and powerless. Your life might be cluttered by a number of things: regret, anger, guilt, judgment, etc.

Let's examine a few ...

> * **REGRET:** Many of you live with regret in the attic of your soul. Regret is about mourning a missed opportunity, about wishing it could have been done differently. But no matter how much regret you have,

**you can't go back and do it again**. All you can do is go forward. How do you do that? By releasing whatever regrets you have. When you do that, you create room for new things, greater opportunities for growth. You might even discover that the thing for which you've been mourning may show up in a different package—a package better suited for who you are today. If you don't release the regret, you will more than likely miss another opportunity. Release your regret. Make room for Acceptance!

* **ANGER:** Are your fists clenched? Is your heart racing? Is your head pounding? If yes, then anger is your guest. Anger is destructive. If you keep this one in storage, it will turn on you, destroy you. Anger does nothing but cause problems for you and others. It creates illness within your being. It can blind you, deafen you, and cause you to lose control. Anger eats at your insides, gnaws at your mind. Anger keeps you from sleeping, eating, and even driving. When is anger useful? Never. Not uncontrolled anger. Certain anger is healthy, which, if expressed properly, can bring you relief. But I'm talking about anger that causes you to break things, start fights, ruin relationships, etc. Here are some positive steps to take when you start to feel the anger surge through you: 1) Pause and think. 2) Take some deep breaths to relax your body. 3) Stay silent and use that time to reassess the situation. 4) Leave the room

if necessary. 5) Try to see the other person's point of view. 6) Move your body; take a walk if needed. 7) Relax your heart and let go. Release your anger. Make room for Peace! At this point, you'll be able to handle the situation in a more composed manner.

*Release brings serenity.*

\* **GUILT:** This is something worth sweeping out of your life. Guilt is a complete waste of time and energy. Guilt often originates when you don't live up to certain expectations. You were brought up to believe that certain things are "good" and that others are "bad." The notion of good and bad are biased; it depends on who you are, from what part of the world you come, what religion you embrace, your age, your gender, etc. So, you do something about which you feel guilty. How does it serve you? If you're feeling guilty over something you did, how long will your sentence be? Even hardened criminals are released after serving their time. If you're feeling guilty about something you're doing now, stop doing it. If you don't, then what's the point of continuing to feel the guilt? It's a waste of energy. It is your way of saying, "Hey, I'm a good person; see, I feel guilty." Sometimes guilt is good. It serves as a moral compass. But do what you need to rectify the situation and move on. Don't hold on to the guilt.

\* **JUDGMENT:** Courtroom is in session. Only you don't get to be judge. Nobody does. It's amazing how quickly human beings tend to judge others, usually for something they themselves do. When you judge others, you define yourself as a person with the need to judge; you don't define the other person. Oftentimes you judge someone simply by his or her appearance. No one truly knows anyone else's circumstances. No one can really know what it is like to be in someone else's shoes. Focus on *your* life, what you can do to grow as a person. Judging others takes away from who you are. Next time you see something you don't understand, refrain from judging. You *really* don't understand. Release your judgment. Make room for Openness.

"Breathe through it
and release anything that does not serve you."

~Unknown

# CHOOSE to RELEASE.

\*\*\*

## *EXERCISE*

Time for that box I mentioned earlier. Today, see if there's anything else you can work on releasing from your life. Here are some ideas:

1) Negativity

2) Self-demeaning thoughts

3) Jealousy

4) Insecurity

5) Resentment

6) Old pain

7) Rigidity

8) Destructive behaviors

9) Fear

Write each of the above items on a separate piece of paper. Pick one. Write out how it governs your life. Drop it in the box. Once you've gone through all of them, release the box. Let it be picked up on trash day. Release the mental and physical clutter from your life. You will be surprised at how good you start to feel.

# Sacrifice

*Sacrifice: the key to your freedom.*

All right, go get a towel. It's time to sweat, to work for what you want. Many of you live in a world of instant gratification. You don't want to wait. You want things yesterday. And if not yesterday, then today or tomorrow, but as soon as possible.

Success has a price. Anything you want—be it material wealth, physical fitness, or emotional well-being—should come with a warning attached to it: *Pay now or pay later, but pay you will!* There are no shortcuts! Today's sacrifice opts you a more fulfilling tomorrow. Worthwhile ventures require work. Let's take material wealth, for example. Sure you could win the lotto, but that may not be in the cards. So what's left? Hard work and sacrifice! You may have to work longer hours. You might even need additional training. Sacrificing may require your time, energy, and money. It may mean taxing your mind and body. If you do the work, however, you will enjoy the benefits.

An old proverb says, *Patience is a bitter plant, but it has sweet fruit.* Patience is the key to getting what you want. Nothing of value is achieved overnight. Whatever you desire, you can have (within reason, obviously). You may be 5' 8" and want to be 6' 0". Not much you can do there. I'm talking about the things within your grasp.

Whatever you want to become, you can be. All it takes is SACRIFICE!

> *Choose to sacrifice in order to gain.*
> *You'll gain more than you sacrifice.*

Think about what it is you want out of life. What is it you have to do to get it? Are you willing to pay the price of success, or have the debt of failure? Getting what you want is a full-time position. You might get tired. In fact, you probably will. Motivate yourself by always keeping the vision of what you want clear in your mind's eye.

I've known several people who have wanted to pursue their dreams, but they kept themselves from attaining them by saying, "I'd like to go back to school, but it will take too long. I'm 30 now, and I'll be 38 when I get done." My response is always the same, "And how old will you be if you don't go to school?"

Sacrificing yourself for a greater good may not always be fun. There were many nights when I was driving home from Antioch University at 10:30 p.m. (I was working on my masters in psychology) when I'd think, *Is this worth it? Three more years of this?* But I never once thought about quitting. I just kept going, doing the work, and one day it was over and I had my degree. No, it wasn't always fun. It was a lot of hard work, but boy, it sure paid off. When my husband decided to start his own home elevator installation and repair business, it was scary. He had to leave behind the security of the job he had. It was quite difficult for many years—

few jobs, slow-paying customers, and growing debt to keep the business alive, all this during our country's economic breakdown. Many days, especially when I saw the debt pile grow ever larger, I would be filled with doubt. When I would ask my husband what kept him energized and going, he would say, "It's all we have; it's what I love, and we're not giving up!" Well, it paid off— the hard work, the long hours, the patience, and the persistence. We now have many jobs, a crew of six, and good-paying customers.

You must decide what you want and how badly you want it. If you want it desperately enough, then the sacrifice required will just be part of the journey—the bitter pill you must swallow to get the results you want.

In order to achieve success, you must **STICK IT OUT**! Make the sacrifice. Commit yourself to succeeding. Become wedded to your dream. Let nothing come between you and IT—not hard work, not long hours, not even loneliness. The more complex your goal, the more difficult your path will be. Nothing but a full commitment on your part is acceptable. Obstacles are a part of any road to success. Don't let them scare you. Resolve to do your best, for as long as necessary. Remember—you can't fail unless you give up.

"The road to success comes through hard work, determination, and sacrifice."

~Dolzinski

# CHOOSE to SACRIFICE!

***

## *EXERCISE*

1) This week, choose to sacrifice something for the long-term greater good. It might be losing a pound by denying yourself that piece of cheesecake.

2) Sacrifice going out in order to finish a project that will further you in your dream.

3) Make a list of things you want to accomplish. What must you sacrifice to attain them?

# Teach

*When you teach, you learn what you teach.*

Recess is over. Class is once again in session. This time, however, you get to teach! You won't need any special credentials. You already have what you need. Teaching is not an occupation as much as it is a way of life. You're already a highly qualified teacher. Every time you interact with another person, you are both a student and a teacher. You may be thinking, *I don't have anything to teach. I barely got through high school.* While a well-rounded education is important, highly recommended even, being a true teacher does not require any special test-taking ability or degree. The only requirement is that you're part of life.

I have a neighbor who I consider a bit off. She's intrusive and into everyone else's business. She has called the police multiple times in the past because someone coughed too loudly, or because kids were playing football in the street, or because someone parked in front of her house (a public street). Yeah, she's peculiar. But she is a great teacher. Why? Because she's taught me a lot about myself. She's taught me that I was too quick to judge her eccentricities; I really don't know her or her past. She's taught me to keep calm despite the fact she's caused our family a great deal of annoyance and duress. She's taught me that we have to be tolerant, even of people who behave in unusual ways, that we must have patience, and that we have to accept what we can't change. Would I have chosen her as a teacher? No, but life did, so I became a student by default.

You teach every day—often without even being aware that you're doing so. Some of the things you teach may surprise you. Here's another example: Imagine it's Christmas time. You're in a long line at a popular store that's getting ready to close. It's finally your turn to pay for those cool jeans after which you've been lusting. You hand over your credit card and, much to your shock, it's maxed out. In a panic, you desperately search for another credit card, your debit card, cash, anything. You hear some grumbling behind you. The sales clerk gives you a subtle but obviously annoyed look. You start to break out in a sweat. What, you wonder, could you possibly be teaching? PATIENCE, my dear, PATIENCE! I've been in both situations. I've felt bad holding up the line; and as the person in line waiting, I've become very impatient and thought, *Why did I pick this line?* Nowadays I find it a good opportunity to practice being patient. Getting antsy won't change a thing, so I relax and just wait, avoiding all negative thoughts about my time being wasted. Any situation can teach us, if we're open. The best way to learn patience is to be in a situation that forces us to be patient. Practice not getting upset and letting your thoughts get the best of you.

You teach many different people in a variety of ways. It's not necessary to sit behind a desk or stand behind a podium. In fact, often the greatest teaching opportunities present themselves when they are least expected, in the largest classroom of all: Earth.

*When you teach, you change lives.*

There are a great many things you can teach. Let's take leadership, for example. How do you teach great leadership? By becoming a great leader. As a writer, one of the key phrases with which I'm quite familiar is *SHOW, DON'T TELL!* Teaching through modeling is one of the most genuine and effective ways to teach. One of the greatest teachers of the 20th century was Mahatma Gandhi. Gandhi taught nonviolence. He believed the only way to stop violence was to demonstrate nonviolence. He taught this through passive resistance (e.g., hunger strikes, boycotts, noncooperation, marches, etc.). Gandhi is quoted as saying, "Nonviolence cannot be preached. It has to be practiced."

You don't have to be Gandhi to teach or to make a difference in the world. All you have to be is you. Another thing you can teach by example is **Tolerance**. You teach tolerance when you accept differences; when you open yourself up to a wide range of beliefs, lifestyles, religions, and allow each individual the freedom of expression, even though your way might be different. Teach tolerance through your own expression of acceptance and empathy. Through tolerance you also teach **Love**.

In order to teach love, start by loving yourself, your family, and your neighbors—everyone with whom you come in contact. Love nature, all plants and animals. Contribute to their preservation. Teach love by being loving.

*Know what you teach, and teach what you know.*

You are teaching and learning continuously. It is a cycle that never ends. Everyone has something to learn as well as to teach. Even the criminal you condemn has something to teach you. He may teach you about the different aspects of humanity, desperation, fear, and forgiveness. The problematic neighbor may teach you about setting boundaries, being more assertive, and peaceful conflict resolution. The homeless person at the freeway entrance may teach you humility, kindness, and gratitude. The teaching never stops. Choose to *teach*!

Open yourself up to the teaching possibilities that exist. Each day notice what you do. What are you teaching? Choose your lessons well.

"In learning you will teach, and in teaching you will learn."

~Phil Collins

# CHOOSE to T*EACH.*

## *EXERCISE*

Each day this week, choose one or all of these:

1) Teach love. Be loving.
2) Teach compassion. Be compassionate.
3) Teach humility. Be humble.
4) Teach empathy. Be empathetic.
5) Teach tolerance. Be tolerant.

# U*se*

*Use yourself as a tool to make a difference.*

There is a phrase commonly heard and coined by Charles Dederich: "Today is the first day of the rest of your life." It's true. With each new day, you get the opportunity to be of use in some way, to make a dent in the world.

When a celebrity is chosen to get a star on The Hollywood Walk of Fame (one of the world's most famous sidewalks), it's a way of recognizing their talent. You might not ever get a star on that well-known sidewalk, but you can still do something that deserves a star. Your worth is often determined by how you use yourself—your talents, your skills, your money, etc. Sometimes you choose to sit back, your worth wasted, like undiscovered treasure. Then you wonder why you lack energy and fail to thrive. Being of use not only improves the quality of your life, it enhances the quality of life of those around you.

How can *you* put yourself to use? In your home? Your community? Your work place? Your world? You have unlimited resources to be the someone you want to be. Do you choose to use yourself as a resource, or do you allow yourself to snooze?

Look around you. Where can you be of service? How can you use yourself in the best way possible?

Take some time to figure this out. When you put yourself to use and make a difference, you will feel needed, valuable, a part of the whole, and a lot more fulfilled. You don't have to stop world hunger—simple, ordinary tasks will do. My dad is one of those people who constantly puts himself to use. I recently told him about my sunglasses feeling too loose on my face. Within a couple of days, he'd purchased some special compound and fixed them. He looks for a need and fills it. The amazing thing is that there's always something. A loose screw that needs to be tightened, a door lock that won't lock, or a wall that needs to be retouched. Because he is always putting himself to use, he feels useful and necessary, and at 86, that's a great thing.

Putting yourself to use requires desire, effort, and a willingness to be productive in your home, community, and on a grander scale, your planet. When you choose to use yourself for some valuable purpose, you choose to deepen the meaning of your life. You choose to have pride, to complement your worth. Are you doing everything you can to make your life and the lives of others better?

*Use yourself whenever you can. Find a void. Fill it.*

There are thousands of ways in which you can put yourself to use. Here are just a few: Give someone a ride who doesn't have a car. Watch your neighbor's child while they run errands. Watch your neighbor's pet while they go on vacation. Report suspicious activity in your neighborhood. Pick up medicine for a sick friend. Take goodies to work in the morning for your coworkers. Do the dishes when it's not your turn. Visit or call people who are lonely. Read to people who can't read. Help clean up graffiti. Pick up the mail and newspaper for someone on vacation. As you can see, it doesn't have to be something huge, just supportive and loving.

*Wake up from your slumber.*
*Let the world know you're alive. Be of use.*

Make your stay on Earth worthwhile, for you and others. Use yourself to make a difference. Imagine coasting through life, your energy wasted. Now imagine opening yourself up to giving, to helping people's lives become a little easier. In addition to being active on Youtropolis.com (an inspirational website where you can help others on many levels and find help for yourself), I just recently started doing live broadcasts on Periscope. It's one of my favorite ways of giving back. I talk about pertinent issues and allow people to ask questions about things that are troubling them. I make sure they have access to me on Twitter and Facebook, as well as on Youtropolis, just in case they need a little extra help. That's a satisfying way for me to be useful and help people at the same time.

You want to get noticed? It's easy when you give of yourself. Put yourself to good use. When you do so, you benefit just as much as the person whom you're helping. What do you have to offer? There is something. Discover what that something is. Opportunity is always knocking. Choose to answer.

*Become a spoke in the wheel of life.*

Here are some questions that may help you figure out how you can use yourself to make a difference: What are your talents? What is it you do well? What do you love to do? (Give this some thought.) Where can you help? How can you improve the lives of others? Remember, in helping to improve the lives of others, you improve yours. We are an interdependent species. Whatever you do for others, you do for yourself.

Don't allow passivity to set in. Make your time count. Be active in life. Use yourself. Know it's the little things, when done from the heart, that count.

"Life is a one-time offer. USE it well."

~Unknown

# CHOOSE to put yourself to USE!

\*\*\*

## *EXERCISE*

This week, find a way to use yourself in a positive way. Pay attention. The opportunity will present itself. Where and how can you make a difference? It can be as simple as giving somebody the right of way on the street or freeway, or helping someone troubleshoot a computer problem. Sometimes it's that easy. Think of how much you're helping. Don't you appreciate it when people do things for you?

# **V***olunteer*

*Volunteering: The gift of love!*

I would venture to say that your days are busy, filled with things to do, places to go, and people to see. Most of you are so wrapped up in your own lives, you forget there is an "out there" where volunteers are needed. Step back. Look beyond your needs and wants.

To volunteer is to donate your time, unconditionally. You can make a difference in your community, in a single human being's life. Volunteering can be done in a number of different ways, in countless organizations. My daughter-in-law, Michelle, volunteers her time by being the Neighborhood Captain. She facilitates monthly meetings with all her neighbors in order to keep the neighborhood safer. By enlisting the help of the local sheriff, she makes sure they are well-informed and better protected. My son Josh volunteers his woodworking abilities by making furniture and other accessories for friends. My parents volunteer to take my mail to the post office when I'm working so I don't have to stop what I'm doing. There are so many different ways that you can donate your time.

Why volunteer? One of the most important reasons is that there is a huge need in our society but not enough people to fill that need. *You* can be one of the people who create meaningful and positive change.

Aside from helping others who are less fortunate than you, there are personal benefits from being a volunteer. Studies have shown that volunteers live longer. According to Mark Snyder, a psychologist and head of the Center for the Study of the Individual and Society at the University of Minnesota, "People who volunteer tend to have higher self-esteem, psychological well-being, and happiness." When you take the time to help someone else, you feel better about yourself. Several of the clients I used to treat told me they had low self-esteem. They expected *me* to make them feel good about themselves. What they didn't realize was that self-esteem couldn't be given to them. Self-esteem comes from doing something that makes you feel proud and accomplished. Only you, personally, can do that.

When you volunteer, you demonstrate your willingness to be unselfish, to give without the thought of monetary gain. When you step into someone else's world, you gain new insight. You also begin to see similar struggles and life situations. You gain a better perspective of what others go through. You learn empathy and compassion. When I spent time volunteering on a hotline at an abused women's shelter, I learned about the plight of these women firsthand. It gave me an appreciation for their hardships. Yes, I knew that battered women had it bad, but actually talking to them and seeing their struggles gave me a clearer picture of their situation. Volunteering is like an exchange of goods—both the volunteer and the receiver are rewarded.

*Allow your unconditional presence*
*to spark hope in someone's life.*

One of life's basic desires is to feel needed. Volunteering fills that need. When you volunteer, you become part of a team, make new friends, learn new things, get to know your community, share a skill, share your time, and add zest to your life. When you volunteer, you touch someone who is lonely, you become a friend, you spice up someone else's life. In the film *The Intern*, starring Robert De Niro and Anne Hathaway, De Niro's character, a retiree with too much free time on his hands, decides to volunteer as an intern at an online fashion site. That decision changes his life. Not only does he help himself by feeling more useful, he also helps his coworkers. He becomes indispensable and someone that people look up to. The results are amazing. Watch the movie! It won't be long before you feel inspired to volunteer.

Volunteering can also be a way of living out your dream. You might be in a dead-end job, or you might simply want to try something new. Volunteering can be that something. Take a moment to think about what you love to do. Is it writing? Perhaps you can write letters for someone who can't. Is it working with children? Call your local school; they are always in need of volunteers. Do you love to cook? Check out some of the shelters or hospices. Do you love animals?

Check out your local animal shelter. How about working with the elderly? Call your local convalescent home. Many residents have no one to visit them. One day you might be grateful for someone like you. Do you love turn-of-the-century homes? Call your local historical society. Volunteer to be a tour guide. As a docent, you can enjoy the feeling of wearing antique clothing and walking through old homes time and time again.

The opportunities are abundant. You can become a volunteer in almost any organization. Choose your favorite. Experiment with different ones.

"Give of yourself so that others may benefit."

~Rossana Snee

# CHOOSE to VOLUNTEER!

\*\*\*

## EXERCISE

1) Think of something you've always wanted to do.

2) Call up the organization that does it.

3) Find out what it would take to become a volunteer doing what you love to do.

4) Volunteer.

# **W**eed

*Weed out what you no longer need in your life.*
*Make room for the seeds of your future.*

It's time to weed. Get out your gardening tools. Don't worry; you're not going to have to actually get down on your knees and get dirty. You will, however, have to do some work. Weeding can be difficult, but the results can leave you feeling pleased and lighthearted.

Many of you have weeds in your life. The weeds to which I am referring are those things in your life that no longer serve you—a toxic relationship, unhealthy foods, a stressful job, an unhealthy lifestyle, taxing and overwhelming activities, etc. They may cause you to feel unhappy, over-whelmed, fearful, and stressed out. **You don't have to live that way just because you've always lived that way!** Continuing to live like that is the biggest barrier to personal growth. If there are certain things with which you are not happy, change them. Every day you have a new oppor-tunity to do things differently. Think about who you'd like to be. Then weed out those things and people who keep you from being that person.

When I was first learning how to paint, I painted a tree that looked bulky and out of place. I didn't know what to do. No matter how much I tried to fix it, the tree kept getting worse, a total eyesore.

My dad finally came out with a tube of white paint and said, "Paint over it. Get rid of that tree!" With a little trepidation, I painted over the tree. The results were amazing. I felt like I could finally breathe again. I had another chance to make things right and ended up with a pretty decent painting. Sometimes you just have to bring out that tube of white paint and paint over what it is you don't like in your life.

In the plant world, there are weeds that are destructive; they overtake your garden, rendering it unattractive and scant. In the people world, there are those who, like aggressive weeds, are destructive, hold you back, and keep you from living out your life the way you truly want and deserve to.

Take inventory of the people with whom you engage. How do they treat you? Do they respect you and treat you with kindness? Do they make an effort to listen and understand you? If not, it's time to take out your people weeder. There is absolutely no reason for you to be verbally or physically abused, or to be treated other than in a kind and loving way. Some people in your life may cause you to feel bad about yourself; they may try and keep you from reaching your full potential. Again, get your weeder out. Weeding out the negative people in your life is a way of showing self-love, a way of recognizing your value and letting others know how you feel about yourself. How you treat yourself is the way you show others how to treat you. Trust that you know what is best for you. Assess how you feel in your relationships with others. Do you feel good, or do you feel drained, upset, and irritable? If you feel good, continue on; if not, examine the relationship. It may be weeding time. There are times when problematic relationships can be fixed. If so, do the best you can. If not, weed away.

*Weed out the old. Prepare yourself for new growth.*

What else can you weed out of your life? How about projects and activities that tend to overwhelm you, or leave you feeling too tired or without any energy for the more important things in your life? Many of you do things, not because it's something you really want to do, but out of a sense of duty and obligation. In the meantime, you constantly feel stressed out and on edge. In how many of those activities do you really need to participate? Can some of them be weeded out? It's time to check in. Prioritize. What is it that you really enjoy doing? Put that at the top of your list. What things in your life would you prefer to set aside, even if only temporarily? Weed out those things on the bottom of the list. Lighten your load. You're here to have fun as well as to work. Don't put your weeder away just yet. There's more.

When was the last time you went through your closets? Your cupboards? Your garage? I bet there are more things than you can imagine that can be weeded out from each of those storage areas. How can there be room for anything new in your life if it is cluttered with the old? Make room. Start with your closets. What items of clothing have you not worn in the last year? Do you think you ever will? If not, then clear them out. Donate the items to a charitable or nonprofit organization, a homeless shelter, or even a family you know of that may benefit from your donation. Don't let sentiment stand in the way.

Move on to your cupboards. Are there spices that have a 1970s label? Weed them out. Are there boxes and cans of food that you stored in case of an emergency, but the emergency never came? Check their expiration dates. More than likely, the dates have expired. The same goes for medications; I bet you'll find one or two that are outdated. Weed them out. How about your garage? Are you able to walk through it with ease? Or is it an obstacle course, piled with dust-covered boxes whose labels you can't even read? Check it out. Those stored items are probably no longer needed by the *You* you are today.

You have full control of what you keep or what you weed out of your life. Take inventory of what you need to do to be who you want to be.

"Once you weed out the negative,
the positive can bloom."

~Rossana Snee

# CHOOSE to WEED out!

## *EXERCISE*

This week, take inventory of your life. Go through and decide what needs to be weeded out. How about:

1) Your relationships. Are they positive or toxic?

2) Your job. Are you happy or stressed out?

3) Your lifestyle. Is it healthy or overindulgent?

4) Your activities. Do they bring pleasure, or are they too taxing?

# X

*Choose to do. Choose to be. Choose.*

This week, put an **X** next to the particular item you want to work on. For example, next to *Sacrifice*, write down what it is you'd like to sacrifice to reach a certain goal. Maybe it's cutting down on Facebook time so that you can read more.

It can be one or several items. Choose as many as you want. But choose something. Your goal is to eventually have every single item **X**'d off.

____**A**ccept_____.

____**B**ehave_____.

____**C**elebrate_____.

____**D**are_____.

____**E**xercise_____.

____**F**orgive_____.

____**G**ive_____.

____**H**onor_____.

___**I**mprove_____.

___**J**og_____.

___**K**now_____.

___**L**earn_____.

___**M**editate_____.

___**N**otice_____.

___**O**pen_____.

___**P**ersevere_____.

___**Q**uestion_____.

___**R**elease_____.

___**S**acrifice_____.

___**T**each_____.

___**U**se_____.

____**V**_olunteer_____.

___**W**_eed_____.

__**X**_____.

____**Y**_earn_____.

___**Z**_eroIn_____.

***

## *EXERCISE*

After you fill in your choices, keep track of your progress. For example: What or whom did you *Weed* out? Write down your experience for future reference. Do that as often as you can.

# Y*earn*

*To yearn is to think the thought
that becomes realized.*

Are you happy with your life? If you're not, what would it take to get you there? Think about areas in your life where you would like to see some change. Change rarely happens on its own. You normally have to take some type of action if you want anything to be different. It is your yearning for something new that will become your motivation to make the necessary changes in your life—the changes that will enrich you with the joy and happiness that is meant to be yours.

To yearn for something is the first step to realization. Regardless of whether or not you're happy with your life, you all yearn for something. Yearning is the spark that ignites movement and growth. Without yearning, you stay locked in place. Understand, however, that to yearn, in and of itself, is not enough to bring about change. Your yearning has to be followed up with the necessary action.

Quiet yourself for a moment and think about your yearnings. Look at some of the possible areas in your life where you might want to experience something different. How about in your current relationship? Do you yearn for intimacy? If yes, how can you achieve that? Perhaps improving your communication skills would be a good first step. Learn to become a better listener. This is quite a difficult task for many people. It's worth strengthening your listening skills since all people yearn to be understood. When they feel understood, your relationship with them will become stronger. Show a genuine interest in others. Become the friend/spouse/lover you want to have. Self-disclose. Don't underestimate the value of vulnerability. When you open up, others tend to do the same.

What do you yearn for in your personal life? What are your dreams and goals? How can you make them a reality? What calls to you? Take time to discover what that is. You'll feel a yearning deep inside. That will be one indication. When you know what it is you yearn for, take the necessary steps toward achieving it. If it is something for which you've yearned for a while, what has stopped you from getting it? Once you know that, you will be able to make changes to get closer to the thing you want. Maybe you'll need help. Ask for it. Your goals can be attained. Pay close attention to what your heart tells you. Then follow through. Don't let the fact that you haven't pursued your dreams and goals become future regrets. Act now. There is no other moment but NOW.

*Feel your yearning; see it through.*
*Let it carry you to the stars.*

How about at work? For what do you yearn there? Would you like a promotion along with an increase in pay? An easier commute? Better benefits? Or to change your career altogether? All this is possible. Knowing what you want is the first step. Then determine to whom it is you have to talk, or what it is you have to do to start the process of getting one step closer to your goal. Don't let obstacles discourage you. Pretend you're on a track team. Think of how many hurdles you have to jump before finishing the race. You wouldn't quit after the first hurdle, would you? Always keep your goal in mind. Don't let what you yearn for fade away. Keep the flame of desire burning within you.

It doesn't matter for what it is you yearn; know it is attainable. Make your yearning concrete. One way to do this is by writing it down. It's like having a map to guide you. Your map is always right there. You can mark off the goals you've accomplished and keep an eye on the ones remaining. Do you yearn to be more relaxed, easygoing, and calm? Do you yearn to be more social, friendly, and outgoing? More loving, kind, and patient? Who do you want to become? The beauty about life is that you can reinvent yourself every step of the way. As I've stated before, you don't have to be who you've always been. If you're not happy with *you*, change yourself. Will it take work? Absolutely. But what worthwhile venture doesn't?

Many of you might ignore your yearnings; you might even think them crazy, out of reach, or impractical. Thinking these things is *you* limiting yourself from reaching your true potential. Listen to the small, whispering voice within you. That voice is your Guide. It knows your highest good.

Discover your yearning. Go get it. You can make it happen!

"I love those who yearn for the impossible."

~Goethe

# CHOOSE to Y*EARN*.

\*\*\*

## *EXERCISE*

This week, spend at least half an hour of quiet time writing down different yearnings that you may have. Don't edit. Write everything down. Then pick one. Follow through. Don't label anything on the list as impossible. Allow yourself to believe that anything, with enough hard work and perseverance, is possible in one way or another.

Questions to ask yourself:

1) What is my first step?

2) Is there someone I need to call?

3) Do I need to register for school? Write a letter? Buy a book?

Once you know your first step, take it. It will lead you to the second step and so on. Take that step!

# Zero In

*Eliminate distractions; zero in on your dreams.*

It's time for target practice. Put away your bow and arrow, though; all that is required is your **Undivided Attention**. With daily practice, you'll eventually be able to hit the bull's-eye—attain your heart's desire. You might want to consider this last chapter as the homestretch. Like all the previous chapters, this one will also require you to do some personal work. And like all the previous chapters, the rewards will certainly be worth your while. This time around, you are to zero in on whatever it is you want to get out of life, be it a more physically fit body, a house overlooking the ocean, a brand-new car, a well-deserved promotion, the reparation of a certain relation-ship, etc. Remember, do not—in any way, shape, or form—restrict yourself from what you can accomplish. The sky's the limit. Trust that anything on which you focus and invest energy will expand.

If you're like most people, your days start out well-intentioned but somehow end up getting eaten by a slew of distractions. Some distractions are unavoidable, even necessary to address. For instance, on your way to shop for groceries, you notice your car is making a strange sound. Upon closer inspection, you realize you need new brakes. Clearly, this is an emergency situation. A change of plans is definitely needed. Then there is the other kind of distraction, one that is actually used by procrastinators to keep from having to do a certain something. Here's an example: You finally set yourself up to study for tomorrow's test (you actually take more time "setting up" than doing the actual studying), and lo and behold, you get a text. It's a friend wanting to share something she'd read on Facebook. You text about it for an hour. When you're done, you've accomplished nothing on your intended goal list.

In order to achieve anything worthwhile in life, there has to be dedication. Avoiding unnecessary distractions and zeroing in on what you need to do will guarantee success. Most of you do not reach your goals, not because you're not smart or talented enough, but because you allow distractions to come between IT and you.

*Zero in on your goal. Let nothing stand in the way.*

By investing the necessary energy, whatever you want to achieve can be had. Zeroing in on your task will ensure that your task will get done. I know many people who start projects and stop midway at the first distraction, or become interested in something else. After a while, they end up with several projects, all at different stages of completion. Zero in on one thing. Choose something you've always wanted to do. Don't let anyone discourage you. Sometimes distractions come as people who think they know what's better for you than you do.

Actor Harrison Ford, one of the top-notch actors of our time, didn't start out as Bob Falfa in *American Graffiti* or Han Solo in *Star Wars*. When he decided he wanted to pursue acting, a milestone for the fiercely shy young man, he was signed on by Columbia Pictures. After playing in a few bit parts, Ford was told by Columbia he had no talent and was let go. Ford could have given up; he could have chosen to believe the Columbia executives. But he didn't. He took a temporary break, and then zeroed in on what he wanted and went after it. He stayed focused. He went on to star in one of the most iconic movies of our time: *Indiana Jones*.

South Korean pianist Lee Hee-Ah was born with only four fingers. The thumb of her left hand had no bones; yet when she was seven years old, her mother started her on the piano to train her hands. The fact that her fingers couldn't even hold a pencil made this a remarkable feat. In time, the piano became Lee Hee-Ah's love and inspiration. So zeroed in was she, that she worked on one passage of Chopin's "Fantasie-Impromptu" for five years. In 1992, she received the First Prize at the South Korean National Student Music Contest—one of many. Despite her "handicap," she is a concert pianist and can play better than most of us with 10 fingers. This is just one of many more examples.

You can create *your* own story.

What do you want out of life? Don't let logic bark its way into your mind when attempting to answer this question. Pretend there are no obstacles, no one telling you that you're nuts, no money challenges, no location issues, etc. Think about what you really want. You may never have considered this question before, believing it unlikely that you could ever have the good fortune to attain (in this lifetime) your dream. I'm here to tell you that **IT IS POSSIBLE**. Anything is possible. Have you heard of Oprah Winfrey? Who hasn't? She is an inspiration to a lot of people. What you may not know is that Oprah didn't always have it easy. In fact, she was raised in poverty, often wearing potato sack dresses to school that elicited mocking from the other students. If that wasn't bad enough, she had to deal with being sexually abused at a very early age. Yet despite it all, Oprah is quoted as saying, "The biggest adventure you can ever take is to live the life of your dreams."

In order for any possibility to become real, you must dedicate yourself to it. Think about how much daily energy you give to other things in your life. You might spend a lot of time thinking about what has happened in your life and what you think is going to happen at some future date. Or perhaps you're constantly on your phone texting; using Twitter, Instagram, or Facebook; or playing Candy Crush. Tally up the hours spent on those activities. Now take all that time and use it to pursue your dream. Imagine what you will be able to accomplish.

Center yourself. Zero in on what it is you desire to get out of life. Remember, if you want to eat an orange, you must peel it first, and then break it off into sections. You must do the same with your dream. What is it you want? Zero in. Take it one step at a time. Don't give up until it's yours.

"Ignore the noise. Zero in on what matters most. Watch it expand."

~Rossana Snee

# **CHOOSE** to **Z***ERO IN* on your heart's desire!

*** 

## *EXERCISE*

Today, practice zeroing in on just one thing. It doesn't have to be a complicated task. Make a commitment to yourself. Do not allow yourself to get distracted. Complete whatever it is you've chosen to do, whether it be reading a chapter in a book, balancing your checkbook, making a call, or sending an important e-mail. Once you've mastered it, move on. Commit to a bigger project.

**List of projects I want to complete**:

Today:

_____

_____

Next Week:

_____

_____

Next Month:

_____

_____

Long-Term Goals:

_____

_____

# Afterword~

We are the actors behind the curtain of our lives. Choose your parts carefully. The things we do, the thoughts we think, and the decisions we make all contribute to the way our lives unfold. **CHOOSE** to enhance the miracle you already are. Make a difference—in your life and in the life of those around you. We are reflections of the choices we make. So choose well.

**A**CCEPT yourself. You are unique and special.

**B**EHAVE kind-heartedly. What if someone were watching? **C**ELEBRATE life. Take nothing for granted. **D**ARE to be you. You are magnificent.

**E**XERCISE often. Keep your body fit and agile.

**F**ORGIVE others. Forgive yourself. It's the only way to truly heal. **G**IVE of yourself and of your time; it's the best gift you have to offer. **H**ONOR yourself. You are priceless. **I**MPROVE what you can; you are a work in progress. **J**OG yourself awake. Live every minute of life the best way you can. **K**NOW that you are special. Let it show. **L**EARN all you can. Never stop. Let knowledge be your sustenance. **M**EDITATE. Calm your soul, soothe your mind, and free your spirit. **N**OTICE details; they make up the whole. Embrace the beauty. **O**PEN yourself to new experiences, new people, and new places. **P**ERSEVERE in all your pursuits. It's the only way to realize them. **Q**UESTION. It will move you forward. **R**ELEASE the hurtful things in your life. Feel the healing begin. **S**ACRIFICE in order to gain riches—both physically and spiritually. You will! **T**EACH what you want to learn. You'll learn even more. **U**SE yourself to make a difference. You can. Don't waste your potential. **V**OLUNTEER. You can make a difference by donating your time to those who need it most. **W***EED* out what you no longer need. Make room for new opportunities. **X**___ Choose to do. Choose to be. But choose. **Y***EARN.* Then go for it. It can be yours. **Z***ERO IN* on your desires. Whatever you focus on grows bigger and more noticeable. Make sure it's your dream.

It is your choice. **CHOOSE** to be the very best you can be!